# JUST
# IMAGINE

# Just Imagine

by
JEWELLE LEWIS

St. James Publishing

**Canadian Cataloguing in Publication Data**

Lewis, Jewelle 1953 -
Just Imagine

ISBN 1-55056-354-8

Published by
St. James Publishing
Box 891
Salmon Arm, BC V1E 4N9
Canada

First Printing 1995

Typeset by the Vancouver Desktop Publishing Centre Ltd.

Printed and bound in Canada by
Friesen Printers a Division of D.W. Friesen & Sons Ltd.
Altona, Manitoba R0G 0B0
Canada

# Acknowledgements

Thanks:

To Ros Staker and Ann Boxall; words cannot express my gratitude for your years of love, encouragement and friendship.

To my friends who have seen me through the stages of this book (and numerous other crisis!); for believing in me, for your love: Patti Allen, Dihane Higgins, Joan Holtzer, Gerry Farren, Gabrielle Hucker, Janine Kohlman, Joyce Shmyr, Karen Williams-Spencer, Maureen Wallin, Sara Watson and Herma Worman.

To my family who gave beyond the call of duty; Bob Lewis, Vivianne Lea and Hank Walle, Korinn Walle, Lillyean Walle, and Konni and Larry Frazier.

With love to Kristy Lewis, Joanne Lewis and Mike Lewis; you are the love of my present life.

With love to Troy Rauhala, my son, my friend.

To Dayle Sheridan; who understands this story more than anyone; who taught me to listen to the whispers of my soul.

To psychics extraordinaire; Dan Valkos, Laara Bracken, Petula Stowell, Becky Webber and Sophie Young.

To members of the Revelstoke Genealogical Society; for sharing with me your knowledge of ancient England, and more.

To my literary agent, Sharon Jarvis, for three years of sound advice and encouragement.

To John F. Garden; you are an inspiration.

To Ingrid Nelson and Shannon Johnston; thanks for the last mile!

Permission granted from Fraser Valley Record, Mission, B.C. for the reproduction of the editorial on John Lennon.

Permission granted from Dr. Juliet Barker, author of "The Bronte Yearbook" for use of the poem written by Emily Jane Bronte.

*To Konni*

# One

"So you think you've lived a past life with John Lennon?" my husband, Bob, would ask.

Sensible, level-headed Bob.

I would answer his question with my usual question, "Well, can you explain all of this?"

I always hoped he could explain because I certainly couldn't. I hoped someone, anyone, could explain.

But a life with John Lennon? I'll let you be the judge.

It all started December 9, 1980, the day after John Lennon was shot.

The stillness of that early morning was interrupted only by the irregular sound of perking coffee. I always savoured these quiet moments before the flurry of getting kids ready for school.

I recall flipping on the radio and as 'White Christmas' played softly, I stood at the kitchen window and watched the lightly falling snow. I was once again caught up in the anticipation of the approaching Christmas season. With the end of the Irving Berlin melody, the news announcer broke into the Yuletide mood with the 7:00 a.m. news.

"John Lennon was fatally shot last evening in New York City just before 11 o'clock. Lennon's wife, Yoko Ono, was with him at the time of the shooting, which occurred just outside their home at the Dakota Apartments. Mark David Chapman, who claimed to be a fan of the ex-Beatle, is being held in custody and has been charged with the shooting. No further details are known at this time."

I recall thinking, 'John Lennon...New York...so that's where you've been' and my head spun as I mechanically got my children off to school.

Images of my own childhood flashed before me. My summer friend, Daphne, and me sitting on a North Shuswap Lake beach, one hot August afternoon in 1964, planning a trip to Vancouver to see the Beatles. I was only eleven years old; the great disappointment of not being able to go soon forgotten amidst the other activities of that summer. Only now, years later, I found myself thinking about it.

My thoughts were erratic. 'New York...why didn't I find that out...before it was too late? Why haven't I been paying attention to where he has been?' Inexplicable thoughts of grief, desperation and loss washed over me, leaving me drained and confused.

The radio stations played a mixture of Christmas carols and Beatles' music. It had been so long since I had heard the Beatles' hits and most of John Lennon's music was new to me.

Later, I huddled at the end of the sofa, hugging my knees and staring into space. John Lennon's 'In My Life' filled the room. An ache penetrated my being so deeply that I thought I would die. Tears slid down my cheeks. My mind went numb. While C-FMI continued to send out it's musical tributes to the slain John Lennon, I wept, and time stood still. My sobbing eventually subsided and I drifted off to sleep.

I was vaguely aware of my husband, Bob, entering the foyer, brushing the snow from his hair. The only noise came from the radio. I heard him turn it off. Bob's warm hand was on my cheek and his voice expressed concern.

"You O.K.?"

I blurted out, "John Lennon was shot!"

He nodded, "Yeah, I heard."

I tried to explain. "I just feel so sad. I haven't thought of the Beatles since I was a kid and I guess it brought back some

memories of when I was young or something...I don't know."
I was feeling self-conscious. "I really don't know why it has hit
me this way."

Suddenly, the children burst in through the double doors,
laughing and fighting at the same time. Flinging coats and snow
covered mittens about, they made a bee line to the kitchen,
emerging with mouths and hands full of cookies.

Bob suggested that we get our Christmas tree before the snow
was too thick to see anything. I agreed, not wanting to admit that
I hadn't noticed the unusually heavy snowfall. As kids piled
noisily into the car, I couldn't help getting caught up in their
excitement as we set out to find the perfect tree.

As we drove through the snow packed streets it was easy to
see the evidence of the day's snowfall. Clumps of fresh snow hung
everywhere, hiding the blemishes of modern day living. Leaving
the small town behind, we were in the country while farm upon
farm became an endless sea of white.

As we did every Christmas, we left the main highway and
headed toward a small forest at the base of a mountain edging
our valley.

Bob became a lumberjack for the time it took to find the
perfectly shaped tree. Critically, he eyed tree after tree, knocking
the heavy snow off each, to make just the right choice. The
children screeched with delight as each one shed its billowing
snowy shower. With nightfall quickly approaching, they were
content to begin the journey home with the promise of hot
chocolate awaiting. I felt safe and warm as we sped through the
night; the branches of our tree bouncing and brushing rhythmi-
cally against the car's roof and windows. The interior was filled
with the sweet aroma of spruce from the resin on the warm mitts
and jackets.

Bob switched on the car radio and we drove through the snowy
night accompanied by the strains of 'Silent Night'.

Unannounced, John Lennon's haunting voice filled the car
with 'Starting Over'. I had to stare fixedly out of the window into
the darkness so that Bob wouldn't notice my sudden tears.

Two days later, the shock and grief seemed to have subsided.

I was aware of Bob watching me as I seemed absorbed in the Christmas preparations. Actually, I was chastising myself for wasting those precious days before Christmas, grieving for a rock star I hadn't thought about for over fifteen years. 'Dammit, what's the matter with me? He was a rock star ... not part of my world. I had to get my act together!'

The next morning I felt my usual self. Minutes after the children had devoured stacks of pancakes and left for school, I wrapped a Christmas parcel and felt glad everything was back to normal. I drove to the mall, light heartedly making a mental list of Christmas chores that needed attention.

At the mall, my first stop was at a small postal counter in the drug store. As I waited my turn in line, I heard John Lennon's 'Woman' being played on the store's sound system. Suddenly I felt ill. The clerk took my parcel and placed it on the scale, pushing the weights this way and that. I had to escape the music. Angry and nauseated, I grabbed the parcel, snapping at the clerk, "Oh, forget it! I'll take it to the main post office where they know what they're doing."

Not caring that people were staring at me, I bolted for the door, jumped in my car and headed downtown. 'Woman' pursued me from the car radio that I didn't think to silence. Oblivious to the tears streaming down my face, I wove in and out of traffic. Suddenly there were two elderly women in a crosswalk in front of me. I slammed on the brakes; the car slid for endless seconds on an icy patch. The two women, laughing and chattering, walked on, totally unaware of me.

From inside my closed car, I screamed at them and the world, "Why are you so happy? Don't you care that John Lennon is dead?" Shaken, I sat for a moment until, from behind me, the blare of a car's honking brought me to my senses. As I moved again with the flow of traffic, I resolved once again to get myself together.

# Two

I was still shaking as I reached the end of our long driveway and found sanctuary in my kitchen. I was just beginning to relax with a steaming cup of tea when the telephone rang. It was an old friend inviting herself over for a visit. Mechanically I agreed; but not really wanting company that afternoon.

Unintentionally, I lapsed into a reverie about that period of my life, ten years earlier when I met Debbie.

Just days after my sixteenth birthday, scared as Hell, I enrolled in R.S.S. I had never seen a school so enormous; nor had I ever been the new kid at school. At my home high school, (to quote my Mom) I had exhibited more interest in partying than in studying and had started running with the wrong crowd. Finally, my parents sent me to live with an aunt. To be allowed back home I would have to change my ways. The school counselor assigned Debbie to introduce me to the way of the school; show me the ropes. I was so relieved to have her help that I didn't complain that this girl didn't seem to be my type.

Debbie had a plump figure, wore her hair long and straight and projected an air of know-it-all superiority. Being in charge of the "new girl" swelled her self- importance. Smiling at everyone, Debbie took great pains to fill me in on the backgrounds of most students; I was amused and entertained by Debbie's analysis of her class mates. I soon learned her opinion of who was worth knowing and who wasn't; who were partiers; who wore their skirts too short or their hair too long.

One day as we filled in time between classes, a tall muscular boy with warm blue eyes strolled along the hallway in our direction. When he spotted me, he widened his eyes and mockingly gave me an exaggerated grin. I turned to watch after he passed only to see him walking backwards, still smiling at me. I burst out laughing and asked Debbie, "Who was that?"

Debbie was very serious in her reply, saying that his name was Patrick White, that he was crazy and that I should stay away from him. She clearly bristled at my amusement of this analysis. In the meantime I was thinking that maybe R.S.S. wouldn't be so bad after all.

To my disappointment, Patrick only occasionally attended school and when I questioned Debbie about how he got away with skipping so many days, she testily replied that he got straight A's and the principal likely felt that anybody who could do that by coming to school once a week deserved to come and go as he pleased.

One day, as Debbie and I were leaving school, a motor- cycle roared through the parking lot, weaving it's noisy path through the parked and mobile cars and screeched to a stop beside us. To my delight, when the cyclist removed his helmet, there was Patrick and he was asking me to go for a spin. Without hesitating, I clambered on behind him, he plopped the helmet on my head and we were off with a jerk and a quick acceleration which made my eyes water. We cut a corner on the bias, narrowly missing an oncoming school bus. Strangely, as I clung to his leather jacket, I felt protected by this spirited young man.

Throughout my high school days Debbie and I remained friends; even when I moved away to have my baby. My son. Patrick's son.

I lost my son through adoption and later I lost Patrick through death.

Forcing myself back to the present, I dialed Debbie's number.

I abruptly gave her the excuse that I was not feeling well, and promised to meet on another day.

Later that evening, I took a hot bubbly bath, accompanied by my newspaper, the *Fraser Valley Record*. As I lay back in anticipation of welcome relaxation, I spotted the headline, "John Lennon: Was He Really So Great?"

# Three

The article which caught my attention accompanied the announcement that a travelling evangelistic preacher, Reverend Tom Allen was to speak on the topic, "John Lennon: Was He Really So Great?" This travelling man of the cloth would appear in the Fraser Valley Church next week. My eyes quickly scanned the article, and I couldn't believe some of the Reverend's opinions:

– Lennon and the Beatles through their music were responsible for promoting such modern maladies as sexual immorality, drug addiction, revolutionary politics and Eastern religions.

– The mood and theme of those years of Beatlemania were simple: *sex*. With songs 'Love Me Do,' 'Please, Please Me' and 'She Loves You,' these four men set an immoral course for North America.

– How can a man live his life promoting sexual immorality, revolutionary politics and Eastern religions, only to be hailed as a hero when he dies?

– Certainly his violent death can be connected with the judgement of God. Lennon lived his entire life in rejection of authority figures, and was shot to death by a young man who had no respect for authority either.

8

– This very day there is no heaven for John Lennon. He has gone to meet his Creator.

– Lennon will meet eternal death in a place called Hell.

– There will be more, of course, on Sunday, when the topic will be 'Rock and Roll, the Bible and the Mind'.

I was furious. I jumped out of the tub, splashing water everywhere. Drying myself and throwing on a bathrobe, I flew to the kitchen to collect paper and pen. I switched on the lamp, sat at my end of the sofa and began to write.

"Dear Mr. Editor:

Never has a newspaper article infuriated me as (did) yours on the late John Lennon. Proclaiming that Lennon will face eternal death in Hell and that his violent death was connected to God's judgement . . . does this also apply to Martin Luther King, John Kennedy and other victims of violence?

John Lennon was an advocate of peace and love, which we needed in the 60s and need today more than ever. The Beatles' early music through to Lennon's last works, told of love, not sexual immorality. We cried when John Lennon died because part of us died too. The Beatles taught us there were alternatives to the ideas of former generations and that we could live in peace and harmony with one another. The rest was up to us.

So, please don't use your newspaper to allow others to slander him in the name of the Lord."

Without missing a beat, I recopied my outburst, hastily folded the single sheet of paper and slipped it into an envelope which I sealed and stamped before addressing it to the Mission, B.C. *Fraser Valley Record.*

I was back on my favorite couch, staring unseeingly when it dawned on me that I had never written a letter to a newspaper before; that the very thought of publicly expressing an opinion has always paralyzed me and, oddly, I was doing so now without hesitation.

# *Four*

The Christmas season was over; carols and Beatles' music vacated the airwaves, television had exhausted it's documentaries on John Lennon and magazine covers no longer bore the famous faces of the 'Fab Four'. 1980 had passed into history, taking with it the sensationalism of Lennon's death.

At the usual time one morning the telephone rang. Expecting Debbie home after a Christmas visit to the Okanagan, I quickly poured a cup of coffee and answered the phone. Not wasting a moment, and with an almost accusing tone in her voice, Debbie told me how she had spotted my letter in the *Fraser Valley Record.*

"Since when do you write letters to the Editor . . . since when do *you* care so much about music . . . and since when do you defend people like *John Lennon?*"

When I wrote the letter I really hadn't thought of the reaction it might provoke in the people I knew. I couldn't think of why it would be a big deal. I tried to explain to Debbie that I wasn't defending John Lennon's music . . . only Lennon himself. Though I had to admit to some doubt about what I was defending.

"But why does it matter that I wrote a letter?" I asked.

"That's what I'd like to know, Jewelle! Why did it matter enough to you that you would write to the paper? . . . I mean, he was just a long haired . . . and those silly glasses . . ."

10

I laughed her off. I humoured her, saying I thought John Lennon was cute. That didn't satisfy her and she hung up in a huff. 'Oh well,' I thought, 'she was always opinionated,' and I let it pass.

Weeks passed; the world seemed to forget its loss of a great human being. Little did I realize, at the time, his music and philosophies would live on.

I longed to forget. I was alone with a pain I couldn't comprehend.

For the next three years I quietly hid an unbearable cold empty ache. I lived two lives; one, mother and wife, and the other a compulsive collector of Beatles' and John Lennon music and trivia. Debbie called it 'latent Beatlemania!'

One dreary April afternoon in 1984, I snapped. I had to reach out to someone; but to whom? I would write to Yoko! I bought expensive stationery, a fine new pen and had written "Dear Yoko" before I realized how ridiculous the whole idea was. I felt humiliated. What in Hell was I doing? Had I really lost it; become a lovesick fan? One day I knew I would have to turn to someone . . . but Yoko was not that someone.

Later that wet spring day, I made a purchase that was to be the first step of so many toward understanding. After finishing the essential shopping, I found myself sidetracked to a record shop and I emerged with a copy of the 'Imagine' album. Having never heard it before, I played the record as soon as I got home. Curled up on the sofa, watching the rain driving against the window, I really heard Lennon's songs for the first time. It was when the track of 'Jealous Guy' began that I experienced a vivid recollection of an ancient milestone nestled in rich green grass at the edge of a narrow roadway. Still legible in the darkened granite were the words " . . . miles to London." It was the same image that came to my mind's eye when, as a child in school, I listened to the teacher read the old English story, "Dick Whittington's Cat."

Why was that image evoked by that song? Why had I seen this exact image twice and so clearly? Plausible explanations eluded me but I knew there was someone I could ask, and it was finally time to do just that. I picked up the telephone and dialed my mother's number in Vancouver.

"Grandma's here! Grandma's here!" heralded Mother's arrival the next day. She distributed hugs all around before shedding her coat, whereupon the children pulled her into their rooms where she was bombarded with school projects, stories and all the important happenings in their lives.

My mother, daughter of a lumberjack, had left her parent's rural home on the North Shuswap Lake during World War II. Times were hard for her parents, who had five other children to provide for. Moving to Kamloops, she boarded with strangers and worked for her room and board while attending high school, and she later became a certified teacher. This experience developed her strong will and lifelong self reliance.

My father was attracted to this confident woman, who during their marriage and while raising their children, often taught school to help maintain for us a secure home life. Mother's opinions and beliefs were the guidelines with which we lived. When her interests in spirituality arose, she pursued the art of learning to live a spiritual life with the right vibrations and a clear mind, with the same vigor and determination as she had as a young woman pursuing a career. She was confidant that all our problems could be solved through various mystic means, one of those recognizing problems that could originate from a past life that cluttered our minds in the present.

I always enjoyed our adult to adult conversations. While I had always humoured her and had a passing interest in these concepts of hers, I never thought of applying any of them to my day to day existence.

I remembered how Mom had informed me, shortly after my son, Michael, was born, who he had been in his previous life. She told me what his name had been and that he had lived in Northern California. She said he had belonged to a branch of the same group of people she worked with, learning to clear the mind. And where did she get this information? "From Michael," she said. She explained that she could "talk" telepathically to my two month old son and how he had told Mom who and where he had lived. I tried unsuccessfully to picture Michael's thought waves as I looked at my husky blond haired son, gurgling to himself, as he lay in his crib.

Months after Mom had seen Michael's past she had talked to a lady who edited a small newsletter for this group. She told Mom she remembered writing up a death announcement for this man who was now my son. This story fascinated me but I never had reason to question her in depth about past lives. However, I was now desperate.

The children's excited welcome ran itself out, and my mother and I were finally left alone over cake and coffee. She lost no time in asking me what problem I had that couldn't be discussed over the phone.

Hesitantly, I edged into my story by telling her how I was still feeling sad, three years after John Lennon's death; that I was constantly listening to his music although I had not done so before 1980, that all of this was driving me crazy; maybe there was something to this psychic business which could explain why I had been feeling and acting this way . . . with a feeling of total help-lessness I stopped my rambling.

Mother took a deep breath and closed her eyes. She sat, not moving a muscle, for several minutes, and I was beginning to feel quite silly. She began to speak slowly and with deliberation. "I do see something . . . I see a young girl . . . in England . . . the 1400s . . . betrothed to a man who in this life was John Lennon. He is sick and is taken away . . . he does not return . . . he dies . . . I see a cart coming for him . . . you are most distressed and you die shortly afterward."

Questions buzzed through my mind. "What were our names?"

Mother, still with eyes closed, said, "Your last name was St. James . . ."

"And my name was Katherine and he was John . . . right?" I couldn't believe the name Katherine came to me like it did . . . but as soon as I had uttered it, I knew there was no possibility of any name but Katherine.

"Yes . . . Katherine and John . . . Baron."

"It's near a place . . . sounds like . . . Castlemere."

"And Katherine's father and mother?"

"Her father's name was Robert... Robert St. James."

"Where is this place, Castlemere?"

"England... near Salisbury Plain... I see white cliffs, fog and lush green grass."

Lush green grass! That was what I had seen surrounding the milestone... when I had first listened to 'Jealous Guy'.

"Quick, come with me." And to my mother's surprise I went to the stereo, letting the sounds of 'Jealous Guy' fill the room. "Tell me if you can pick up anything from this song, O.K.?"

When the melody ended, my mother only said, "This song is written about this life in ancient England. He seems to be talking about his death... oh, and I could hear chimes... not in the song but I could hear them in my mind... there were chimes where you lived."

It was as if my three year old cloud had disintegrated and drifted away in a million wisps; everything seemed clearer. I had actually known him. I found myself laughing and crying all at once, asking my mother why I had taken so long to tell her of my grief.

"Everything happens in it's own good time. Three years ago you weren't ready for answers because you didn't know the questions. Besides, people only question Life when they are ready to hear answers."

Therefore, in the spring of 1984, I was now ready to hear answers, to accept that I was once Katherine St. James who had loved a John Baron – but only on one condition: that I could prove it.

# *Five*

On a Sunday afternoon in April, after a late breakfast, I summoned the courage to share with Bob my mother's explanation of my prolonged, inexplicable grief.

Bob stared at me as if I had lost my mind. "Are you saying you are connected to the 'Imagine' album?" he snorted.

"No," I managed despite my wired up nerves, "not the album . . . a song on the album . . . 'Jealous Guy'."

"I don't understand what you're getting at. What, exactly, are you talking about?"

"Mom saw that I had known John Lennon in another life and . . ."

"Well, that explains it, doesn't it? For Christ's sake, Jewelle, she's always got some kooky idea; you can just add this one to the list. As a school teacher you'd think she'd be more realistic about life."

"Look . . . I was the one who asked her if I had known him in another life. It didn't come easy . . . asking her. It's nothing I can touch or see but I feel so . . . Oh, forget it!" I was mumbling and felt humiliated.

By the next day, I had mostly recuperated from Bob's stinging words. I knew that he scoffed at spiritual ideas and that accepting new ideas, with no scientific proof, was impossible for him. And when my mother was the one giving me the information, it was doubly hard to convince him of any validity in the whole thing.

Bob's own upbringing had been with a Naval Petty Officer father who was often away and a mother who raised her children virtually alone, yet in the unseen shadow of her husband's conservative values.

I knew my upbringing had it's equal flaws stemming from my mother's determination that we become as spiritual as humanly possible. My first recollection was eating only health food in a time when it was referred to as being a health food nut. Luckily, I found a friend at school who ate dried kelp at recess and who never drank milk! At age twelve I tried to argue against having to change my name but my mother insisted that we needed the right vibrations. Julie now became Jewelle. My sister, Connie, became Konni.

In my teens Mother connected with a different group of friends who did routine therapy sessions on each other to rid themselves of all past upsets; physical and mental pains. The theory was to clear the mind to allow the person's true and good personality to emerge. After many of Mother's sessions it was apparent that she had developed psychic abilities. She stressed that these were abilities she had always had but because she had gotten rid of her mental "garbage" these abilities were now able to surface more clearly. She also insisted that if everyone cleared their minds, they too would be "naturally" psychic.

Over the years a good portion of our family, including my father, my aunts, cousins and even my grandmother, would talk of extra-ordinary happenings as an everyday order of things.

As a young adult I soon learned that most of the world didn't discuss so openly the reasons why people react the way they do or that maybe most people's problems stem from our soul's past. And when, at age sixteen, I went to live with an aunt who was not spiritually minded, I saw how others lived with down to earth ideals and were still happy with their lives.

So, when Bob openly scoffed at my mother's "kooky ideas", I was once again torn between what I had learned and what a logical person with a more normal upbringing would think.

I was so unsure of myself. Maybe Bob had a point. I may have even agreed with him except I couldn't discount the feelings of loneliness and loss I felt for this man I had never met. I had to prove to myself without a doubt whether I had known and loved the soul most recently known as John Lennon. I wouldn't try to explain anymore to Bob or anyone else until I was able to explain it to myself. After all, it was I who needed to know the truth.

With Bob and the children safely at work and school, I ignored the lure of the early morning sunshine and retreated to a corner of our basement. I blew the dust off of an Atlas of the World and carefully turned pages until I found England. After an hour of tracing my finger over the names of hundreds of cities and villages, searching for Castlemere, blurring vision and an aching back forced me to give up.

With a fresh cup of coffee in hand, I went out into the sunshine. I mentally reviewed and visualized the scene my mother had sketched for me just days earlier . . .

"Medieval English village of Castlemere . . . a young Katherine St. James, daughter of Robert St. James, merchant, had fallen in love with and was to have married John Baron, son of the local gentry. The young couple had spent hours walking in lush green countryside or sitting in the small garden adjacent to the St. James home. Wherever they were, the sound of chimes was always present. Somewhere in the area were white cliffs surrounded by thick grey fog. Shortly before the nuptial date, John fell ill. Arrangements were made for his transport to a rest home. On that last afternoon spent together, Katherine and John sat in the garden, oblivious to the cool October wind, awaiting the cart which was to take him away from her. As the horse drew the cart to a stop, John took Katherine's hand and whispered, 'Please remember . . . always remember our love.'"

There were so few clues. I had no luck finding Castlemere on the map of England. How could I find any trace of the Baron and St. James families if I could not first locate where they had lived?

Impulsively I grabbed my purse and car keys and drove to the public library. There I checked out an armful of books bearing titles like, *Medieval England, History of the British Isles, Life in the Fifteenth Century* and *Lost Villages of Britain.*

I spent the long, hot days of that summer a devoted student of English history. For hours on end, I devoured accounts of past life in England. I entered the worlds of lords and ladies; knights in shining armour; whole class systems living and dying in draughty, cold castles. I sympathized with the lot of the lower classes on whose toil, hunger and suffering, the prosperity of the privileged was built. I learned the stories of Henry the Eighth, Anne Boleyn, Bloody Mary, Elizabeth I, Cromwell, the Plague – all those fascinating stories which somehow slipped by me in school. I loved learning this colourful history but nowhere was there mention of a town called Castlemere or families bearing the names of Baron or St. James.

Then one hot afternoon, late in August, I stuffed the children into the car, surrounded them with stacks of books and headed out for one more trek. While the children were having their daily swim, I struggled into the library with my huge stack of books. The librarian, a kindly older woman, was looking at me, curiosity written all over her face. For some time, she had wondered about why I was checking out so many history books.

"What are you studying?" she asked.

"I'm not studying really ... I'm just trying to find information about some people who lived in medieval times."

"What people?"

"Uh ... ancestors."

Her face lit up, "Oh, you're doing genealogy!" When she saw my puzzled expression, she added, "Family trees."

I jumped at that, still not quite sure what she meant. I was ushered to a shelf of books I had not investigated. At once I saw that it was histories of families rather than histories of a country that I wanted. The librarian was asking what period I was researching. When I told her the 1400s, her eyebrows registered surprise and she confessed having difficulty doing genealogy earlier than the 1700s. How could I explain that I had not gone past any century but had just landed shakily in the 1400s?

"If none of these are of any help, I suggest you phone the Jesus

Christ of Latter Day Saints Historical Society. They have copies of parish records from all over the world and they offer help to anyone who is researching their own families. Genealogists would be lost without them."

Rummaging through her stack of references, she found the telephone number of the Vancouver branch and gave it to me. As an afterthought she added, "We have micro-fiche lent to us by the L.D.S. Church, that you would be welcome to look at." She gestured to a room at the back of the library.

"Any time you would like to look at them, I'll show you how to operate the micro-fiche readers."

On the drive home I was fascinated by the idea of looking at ancient records right there in our local library. But would I find my ancient people? Had they ever existed?

As soon as I got home, I dialed the L.D.S. Church number and attempted to explain my quest to the woman who took my call.

When I spoke of Castlemere, England, in the 1400s, she expressed surprise and said that the books she needed were at her home. After having me repeat the particulars, she requested I phone again in a couple of days and ask for Glynis.

"Oh, and in the meantime, send me your family group sheets. It will help me to know where to begin."

I broke into a sweat. What in Hell were family group sheets?

# *Six*

I sat for some time at my kitchen table agonizing over how I would go about producing family group sheets when I was clueless about what they were. Realizing I had no choice and dreading another dead end, I telephoned Glynis and blurted out, "This is Jewelle...I'm sorry but I wasn't totally honest with you earlier. You see, I am not researching my family tree; I have been told by a psychic that I had lived a past life in England. I'm trying to verify that...and I don't have a clue what those group sheets are! I have been told of a past life near Castlemere, a girl named Katherine St. James, whose father was Robert St. James and a man named John Baron who all lived in England around 1430..."

This was met by laughter from the other end of the line. Then Glynis confessed that after talking to me she had wondered how I had managed to trace my family back to the fifteenth century without previously using their reference facilities.

Glynis explained that family group sheets were a recording of your family tree, starting with yourself and working your way backwards. An expert genealogist would end up with hundreds of "grandparents" over many generations.

I plunged on, asking her if she would still be able to help me. There was a pause before she said, "As a Mormon I'm not supposed to believe in this type of thing but because of my husband, I do." She went on to explain that her husband could describe in detail Moscow's Red Square but because he had never been there, the only logical explanation they had been able to come up with was that he must have been there in a past life. She promised to help all she could and requested a few days to see what she could do.

My watch told me that I had no time to savour this piece of good luck; it was time to fetch the kids from the pool. I was about to leave when the telephone rang. Had Glynis found Castlemere already?

"Hi, what's new?" It was Debbie suggesting that with the kids returning to school on Tuesday, we could spend the day in Vancouver shopping in Gastown and going for lunch. It took me only seconds to agree and set the time.

The 'Back to School Ritual' filled the next few days as I was caught up in the annual foray of readying wardrobes and buying supplies.

One afternoon as I sat in the beauty salon waiting for my girls to have their hair cut, I noticed a poster on the wall announcing that a psychic was coming that evening and sessions could be arranged by appointment. As I paid the stylist for the hair cuts, I hesitantly asked where the psychic was to be. Upon being told, "Right here in the salon," I impulsively made an appointment.

After dinner, nervous and excited, I informed Bob that I was going out for about an hour and that I was seeing a psychic. I hoped he would not question my reasons. He did not.

As I drove through the dark streets to the salon, my mind buzzed with questions to ask. By the time I arrived at the door, however, I found that I had none. What would I say? I could just imagine the reaction to an opening line, "Hi, I am Jewelle, John Lennon's medieval lover. Tell me more!"

The plump, friendly woman who greeted me, motioned me to follow her into a room beyond the salon, where she invited me to sit at a small oval table. While she lit a plain white candle, she introduced herself as Madeline and confirmed that I was Jewelle.

"I've never been to a psychic before." I heard myself saying,

21

"except, of course, my mother...who is psychic...but she's my mother so that doesn't really count does it?" I stopped, lamely realizing that I was babbling.

Madeline smiled as she took my hand, examining the lines in my palm. "Ah, I see a few stormy years when you were in your teens...finding your niche in life. You have developed into a stable well-rounded young lady. Your life with your husband and children is happy and secure. Yet...I see an underlying problem within your heart...you belong with a man from long ago...he is someone you have not connected with for many lifetimes. It is as if you are always in the wrong place at the wrong time. Now ...just a minute...I am getting someone here with you...a male ...Did you have a friend who died in a motorcycle accident?"

"Yes."

"He says to tell you that he is with you and he is trying to help you. Do you understand that message?"

"No."

"He says you will in time."

"...back to this man I am 'connected to'...will I meet him in my next life?"

"You will meet him in **this** life through some sort of meditation."

I thought sardonically, "This lifetime...John Lennon...oh, sure!"

"Do you have any other questions before we finish?"

"Yes, just one...this man...the one I haven't been connecting with...can you see what he was doing in his last life?"

Madeline paused briefly before saying, "I can only see one aspect of his last life...music."

Bob greeted me with, "Well, what did the crystal ball reveal?" in a tone that was at once, both sarcastic and curious.

"Oh, it said I am married to a tall, dark, sexy man who has more brains that money."

"In that case, I'm glad it wasn't a waste of time," he smiled.

I slept soundly that night, quickly entering the hazy world of dreams.

My surroundings became crystal clear; I was walking over soft green rolling fields...someone was holding my hand...it was Patrick!

"I shouldn't be here," he said, "but I wanted to spend a minute with you."

"Patrick, I have missed you...oh, it's good to see you...to hear your voice...are you all right?"

He stared at me, his warm eyes intense, "Jewelle, put foxglove on my grave."

Some men were approaching and, instinctively I knew that Patrick was in danger; he was not supposed to be here.

I screamed for him to run. Instantly, he was gone and the beautiful field with him. Gasping for air, I sat upright.

A cold trickle of sweat worked it's way down my spine. From beside me, I heard Bob groggily asking me what was wrong. I told him I had a dream and then asked him what foxglove was.

"Huh?"

"What's foxglove?"

"A flower."

"Does it grow here?"

"...well, some I guess, but mostly on Vancouver Island...brought there by the British...Jesus, Jewelle! It's four o'clock in the morning."

I lay staring at the ceiling wondering if I had had a dream or had Patrick actually been there? And why had Patrick told me to put foxglove on his grave? How could I have dreamed about a flower I had never heard of? And how could I have remembered exactly how his voice had sounded, after all these years?

# Seven

When Debbie's Camaro turned into the driveway the next morning, I waved good-bye to the children and wished them a good day at school. I hopped into Debbie's car and was glad to see her in a good mood. In unison, we laughingly declared our gratitude for the beginning of school and having survived another summer break. As we cruised along the highway in a companionable silence, I felt a compulsive urge to share details of the experiences I had bottled up for so long.

"I went to a psychic the other day," I started. "...I think I knew John Lennon in another life in England." And before I knew it, I had told the silent Debbie how I had suffered over Lennon's death and how I was trying to find some answers to my nagging questions.

Debbie's face was blank; she registered nothing in response to what I had just spilled out. She was going to tell me I was nuts! Then with a trace of understanding in her voice, Debbie asked, "Is that why you wrote that letter to the paper?"

I shrugged, and then told her about the strange dream I had about Patrick White, saying it was really weird because after all these years, I had forgotten what his voice sounded like.

"What did he say?"

"He told me to put foxglove on his grave."

"That's creepy," Debbie shuddered.

"I know," I said wistfully. "You'd think after all these years, if he was going to contact me he would mention the baby ... I mean, that's our connection, not some flower called foxglove..." I trailed off.

Our conversation turned lighter as we approached downtown Vancouver and, for the first time in months, I felt carefree and frivolous as we browsed our way from shop to shop. Hours later burdened with packages and sore feet, we lucked upon a coffee shop.

"Caesar salad!"

"Cheesecake!"

Seated at an oval table surrounded by real green plants and soft music, we sipped wine and dallied over our sinful choices of salads and desserts. Without warning, tears sprang to my eyes and I broke the relaxed mood. "I've never said this to anyone ... but, I miss John so much sometimes I think I'll die."

Although she was probably thinking, 'for Christ's sake,' Debbie kept a straight face as she said, "It sounds like a puzzle and you have to find all the missing pieces."

I had not thought of it that way and confessed that I had a lot of pieces to find.

"You'll find them," whispered Debbie.

I wondered to myself, 'Is she thinking that my life has become so boring that I am inventing lives with rock stars and teenaged heart throbs?'

As we were about to get into the car, I noticed a small shop on the opposite side of the street. The sign on the window simply read, 'Posters'. For some reason I had to go in. Leaving Debbie standing beside her opened car door, I dodged traffic and dashed into the store. I hastily scanned the racks of posters until I found one with the Beatles. Even though it was of disappointing quality, I took it to the counter. There, an elderly man sitting on a stool looked at my choice, looked intently at me and shuffled to the rear of the store. "Hang on a minute, lady. I have something for you back here." He emerged unrolling another Beatles' poster. This was a beautiful one which commemorated their Royal Command Performance in 1963. "This is for you ... I just got it from New York." Feeling somewhat bewildered, I asked the price, expecting an exorbitant figure. I scarcely believed the five dollar quote and had to ask him to repeat it.

Moments later, I was in the car, both posters securely placed beside me. I was relieved when Debbie turned on the car radio eliminating the need to talk. All the way home I wondered why that storekeeper had kept such a good poster in the back when posters were all he sold . . . and why he had sold it to me for such a low price when the rest were twice the cost?

Later, as I tucked the children into bed, I asked each about their first day at school. Twelve year old Joanne did not want to talk of school. Her pale face bore a puzzled expression. "Mom, someone has been hanging around me . . . just watching me."

How does a mother react to a statement like that from a daughter, no longer a child, but not yet a young woman?

"At school? Damn it, this happens every September at schools . . . did you tell your teacher? I'm going to phone your principal . . ."

"Mom, not at school, here . . . at home . . . it's not a person . . . it is a spirit . . . a man spirit . . ."

Instantly relieved, I had a second to breathe freely before I realized exactly what she had said. "A spirit . . . ?" I had to swallow hard with that one and asked calmly what this "spirit" looked like.

Joanne, in a matter of fact way, stated that he was wearing "spectacles." "He's real small. Well, maybe he just looks small because he's at a distance. Up there," she pointed above our heads.

"Can you see anything else besides spectacles?"

I didn't comment, though I thought spectacles was an old fashioned word for Joanne to use for glasses.

Joanne easily replied, "He has a funny hat. It's a plaid hat with a pom-pom on it. Beige shorts with elastic bottoms, plaid knee high socks and black shoes with buckles."

"Strange outfit," we both laughed.

Joanne suddenly said, "I know the hat. It's like a Sherlock Holmes hat . . . !"

The spirit suddenly seemed a friendly sort, though I wasn't

really convinced there was a spirit. However, it did make light entertainment for a mother whose daughter was beginning that estranged pre-teen age.

"Who is this spirit? Does he have a name?" I asked, humouring her.

"I don't know."

"Well, ask!"

Joanne closed her eyes only for a minute before she replied, "Mom, it's John Lennon!"

# *Eight*

"John Lennon? Are you sure?" I asked, no longer humouring her.

I didn't want to startle her but as I looked at her calm little face, I realized I was the startled one.

"How can you see him?"

"Because he wants me to see him."

"Is he here right now?"

"Yes."

My mind raced. While wanting to grab the moment, I didn't want to frighten or confuse her. As calmly as I could, I explained that I was going to ask her questions (to ask the spirit) for which it was unlikely she would know the answers. Perhaps the John spirit could supply the answers for her.

"Can you tell me the name of John Lennon's mother?"

"... Lia or something sounding like that."

"It was Julia." I supplied. "John had an aunt who raised him. .. can you name her?"

All Joanne could supply was the letter 'M'. "It's like M .. M .. M .." (Lennon's aunt's name is Mimi.)

For the uncle's name she correctly responded, "George!"

"When is John Lennon's birthday?" She indicated July, then October. (John Lennon was born October 9, 1940.)

Although I was amazed that my little girl was giving me the

28

information so effortlessly, I recalled having read about this kind of interview. Perceptive people can, evidently, pick up on the thoughts of the very person questioning them and merely parrot them back. I decided to test this out by asking Joanne questions about my own childhood. "When I was your age, Joanne, and in elementary school, I had a best friend. What was her name?"

Joanne responded with Pamela; the correct answer was Terry. I followed with a similar question about my friend, Daphne, whom I saw only in the summer holidays. Joanne gave me Lisa. After I had asked her a few more related questions, I was sure she was not picking up anything from me. All the questions she had answered about John Lennon had been totally or partially correct but all her responses concerning me were incorrect.

"Is John still here right now?"

At Joanne's nod I asked her if she could tell me anything that would make me believe that he was there.

"Just . . . he hopes you like the poster, Mom."

I was still swallowing hard from that one when Joanne yawned, announcing that she was bored and wanted to go to sleep.

The next morning I turned on my stereo, listening to 'Jealous Guy' and tried to make sense of it all . . .

Over the next few weeks, I would sit with Joanne and ask her questions to ask John. I was totally convinced that her information was coming from John Lennon. Her answers were too wise and her vocabulary was not of a twelve year old.

In this same time period, my mother had been trying to convince me to join her friend's organization. My mom was sure that the way for me to figure out my past lives was to clear my mind of all it's upsets.

Although I accepted her psychic abilities, I wasn't ready to join a group that had a bearing on my childhood quest to remain 'normal'. However, I also had the deep rooted theory that Mother knew best. Torn between my mother's knowledge and my wanting to learn of John and Katherine's past, yet wishing to retain my independence, I posed my questions to Joanne.

"Joanne, would you ask John if I should join up with Grandma's friends ... if it will help me become united with him again. And would it help me to find out more about our English life?"

She simply stated, "He says it doesn't matter whether you join Grandma's friends or not. It doesn't matter what you do, you and he will always be together. And it doesn't matter how you search for your past life. All you have to do is ask to receive the answers."

Another day, I asked her how John was able to reach so many people through his ability to write wonderful music.

"John says, it was his given job. Everybody has a job to do ... but everyone is also given help if they require it. He says he had an ability to write music and to perform ... but some music was 'given' to him." Joanne looked confused, "Mom, how could someone else give him music ... why would they do that?"

I didn't want to tell her that I suspected the 'someone' was a spirit, so I nonchalantly said, "Let's just ask him who gave him this music, O.K.?"

The little girl wrinkled up her face. "John had a teacher who had always helped him with his music. Through his teacher he has grown to love waltzes."

"Does his teacher have a name?"

"Johann."

My mind raced. Waltzes ... Johann ... "Is this Johann Strauss?" I asked Joanne.

Joanne paused for a minute then nonchalantly said, "Yes, Johann says that's how people knew him." The girl looked at me with a puzzled look and said, "Mom, who is this Strauss guy?"

"A man who wrote beautiful music ..." I trailed off.

By now I was getting used to unexpected answers. I suppose I should have been mind boggled over this, but instead I had an overwhelming sense of pride for John and what he had accomplished. I also felt he had more than completed any job that the Universe may have assigned to him.

"One more thing, Mom. Your job is part of this too. Your job is to continue John's work by keeping people aware of him. If they remember him they will also remember the messages he tried to give the world through his music."

I smiled. 'Oh yeah, right,' I thought, 'I'll just be telling everyone that I'm a messenger of John's! Maybe, I'll be more apt to be believed if I say that I've seen Elvis at the local supermarket!'

I started to wonder, what was I supposed to do with this information? Does this happen to people all the time? Do they keep it quiet? Is it meant to be kept quiet? It made me think of the messages in John's music. What use would they have been if he had kept them to himself? Did his music even belong to him? Did my knowledge of these conversations with Joanne or this emerging story belong to me, or were they given to me to share? These questions stayed with me for many years.

One day, a few weeks after Joanne had first "seen" John Lennon, she announced she didn't want to talk with John any more. I had to respect her decision and considered myself lucky for those few precious weeks that I was able to communicate with John, through her.

Finally, I heard from Glynis as the postman brought a big brown envelope. In it were copies of ancient maps of all the English counties. In addition, there was a short history of the origin of the Baron family and a description of the lives of medieval peasants and noblemen. Glynis had included a personal post-script in which she said that she was unable to find 'Castlemere' or a 'St. James' family from that era. She concluded by promising to keep in touch with me.

The deep blue hazy skies of another autumn framed vivid gold trees and the azure mountain sides. Sated with their Thanksgiving dinner, our children had abandoned Bob and me, while we lingered over glasses of wine. I had waited some weeks for this opportunity to catch Bob in a mellow mood. "Bob, I want to go to England."

"Yeah, right!" was his laughing response. When I insisted that I was serious, he held up the bottle and asked me how much wine I'd drank. Determined not to get annoyed, I plunged ahead to say that I did not mean right away, but that I had to go find where Katherine had lived.

Exasperated, he countered, "Where in England? You can't just go over there with no destination. Besides, it will take years to save that kind of money!"

To that, I stubbornly replied that I would save for years if I had to and begged him to try and understand.

The topic was dropped when Bob suggested that we worry about it when I got the money.

Over the next few days, I unsuccessfully tried to think of ways I could earn the money for a trip to England without becoming a working mother. I invited Debbie to come over for coffee with the intention of picking her brains.

"England...why would you want to go to England?" I was taken aback by this reaction. Surely Debbie had understood when I had poured out the whole story to her on our shopping trip? I heard myself quoting her earlier remark about the puzzle I had to put together. "Did I say that?" she asked.

Then the door opened and Bob strode over to the table, laid a large, brown paper wrapped flat parcel in front of me. He kissed me, said "Surprise," and told me to open it. When I ripped away the paper, I found that he had taken my Beatles' poster and had it mounted and framed. He hung it on our oak panelled feature wall where it looked just wonderful to me.

"It looks all right, I guess," remarked Debbie. "Except John Lennon has a real sneer, doesn't he?"

I squinted hard but couldn't see a sneer.

That evening, I telephoned my mother, telling her of my idea to travel to England. She suggested I invite my sister to go along. She meant Korinn, of course. Konni could not manage such a trip.

I have two sisters. Korinn, the younger one, is quiet, easy going and always ready for an adventure. Her sunny disposition matches her fair hair and twinkling deep blue eyes. She didn't know that Mom and I had talked about the current status of her love life, waiting for a wedding. Her modern woman role, however, seemed to suit her just fine.

My sister, Konni, had moved to California after she married an American. We rarely saw her, as Multiple Sclerosis had

32

confined her to her home. It hurt me to visualize her tall thin body confined to a wheelchair and I wondered if she could still manage her long dark hair. Contact with her family in Canada consisted of rare visits and the use of tapes in place of letters.

Mom was right; I wouldn't want to travel alone to another country. Korinn would be perfect. But, why am I thinking about travelling anywhere, when I haven't saved a dime?

My mother, pointing out that my call was costing money, was about to say good-bye but I had something to ask.

"Could you look at something psychically for me? I probably shouldn't have done it," I said, "But I confided my feelings about John Lennon to Debbie back in the fall. She seemed to understand, but today she acted weird. She acted the same way when I wrote a letter to the paper just after he died. She just seems hostile toward him and I don't know why."

My mother said that she 'got the picture' and that she'd be out for a visit soon; we would talk then.

I barely returned the telephone to its rest, when it rang.

Glynis said excitedly, "Jewelle, I have found your Castlemere!"

# Nine

C astlemere existed!

Pent up questions tumbled out of me. Glynis responded by saying that she had been doing research about Stonehenge in the south of England and had come across this passage, in a book written by a lady, Celia Fiennes, who travelled throughout England between 1685-1718.

The passage read, "From Stonidge I went to Evell (Yeovil) in Somersetshire thence to Meer (Mere) a little town; by the town is a vast hill called the Castle of Meer, its now all grass over and so steepe that the ascent is by footsteps cut in the side of the hill ..."

That was why I couldn't locate it. Castlemere was actually the Castle of Mere, located in the town of Mere. Glynis added that Mere borders the Salisbury Plain near Stonehenge in the county of Wiltshire.

I now had a focal point – a destination; all I had to do was find proof that a Katherine St. James or a John Baron had lived there.

For the next several weeks I tried to research Wiltshire in the fifteenth century but other than information on the ancient rings of stone, Stonehenge, there wasn't much.

One day, as I was leaving the small library, I picked up a pamphlet entitled, 'Tracing Your Roots'. Observing me looking at it, the librarian assured me that it was an interesting course in genealogy. It occurred to me that such a course might give me the method of verifying the existence of Katherine St. James and John Baron and their association with Mere.

That evening my mother phoned to tell me she was delaying her visit. Christmas was not that far away; she would come to visit then. With some hesitation, she added that she had taken a psychic look at Debbie's seemingly hostile attitude toward John Lennon and her lack of compassion toward my obvious pain. "I don't like to cause trouble between the two of you. You have been friends for so long . . . and maybe it won't even be of any help."

Not about to get away with that, I demanded details.

" . . . Well, the whole picture wasn't clear but I saw Debbie as having been in the same ancient life as you . . . she seems to have been a house servant for the St. James family. One thing I saw was John waiting for you – for Katherine – in the garden. Debbie (or whoever she was) approached him, making eyes at him. When he just sneered at her and walked away, she was most insulted."

Sneered! That was what Debbie had said when she saw my poster! I explained to Mother about my poster and Debbie's remark about John Lennon sneering.

"Well, I would say that you're dealing with someone who has her own memories of a past life. These memories aren't like the memories you and Debbie share of your old high school days together. Past life memories, if a person isn't aware of what they are, emerge as feelings rather than mental recollections. And sometimes these feelings can be disturbing. Jewelle, remember that unexplainable grief you felt when John Lennon was shot. Well, that was a past life feeling. You had no past memory of having loved and lost but you did have the feelings. This is no different with Debbie. For reasons (probably more than one) beyond her logical control, she feels very uncomfortable when you mention John Lennon. Remember, dear, that our present relationships with others, our feelings, our loves and our hates, often survive the passage of time."

Christmas morning, 1984; Bob and I snuggled under the covers and listened to the squeals of delight as stockings were emptied. I was fumbling about for my slippers when Bob stopped me. Still lying in bed, he had produced a narrow box, wrapped in silver paper. "I want to give you this before we face the mob."

As I opened the parcel, I sensed that Bob somehow was giving this gift to himself as well as me. In the box was a British Airways open return ticket, Vancouver to London. Through my tears, I posed all the obstacles; "Where did he get the money? Who would look after the kids?" With a laugh and a hug, he said, "It's all taken care of; I will book my holidays for September and be a Mom for awhile. Please note that it is a return ticket and you will be coming back." I realized that he hoped that if I made the trip, I would get the whole John Lennon thing out of my system.

I made plans with Korinn, who lived in Vancouver, to accompany me. With months to anticipate our trip, I determined the itinerary so that we would spend the first week in London, playing tourist, followed by travelling to Salisbury, the largest centre near Mere.

I immersed myself in the genealogy course as one way of passing the time. I found the classes hypnotic; the instructor guided us back in time and soon I regarded myself as having been transformed from an amateur, looking for instant answers, to an avid and thorough researcher.

I became educated in my own family's roots. My father's side, Norwegian. My mother's father, Swedish, and my mother's mother who emphatically stressed, "Don't ask me my ancestry: I'm a Canadian." My Grandma reminded us that she was born in Victoria at the turn of the century and how her parents, who were married in B.C., were also born in Canada. "How dare people not accept Canadian as my nationality!"

As the time for our departure grew closer, I found myself thinking of our sister, Konni, whose condition left her confined to her California home. When was the last time I had even talked to her? To help dispel the feelings I had about living a normal life while she was held prisoner by her illness, I got out my tape recorder and began to talk. After a slow start with family news,

I told her about Korinn and me flying to England and I was soon telling Konni my reasons for going and how Mom had seen my past life with John Lennon. Having nothing more to say, I filled the remainder of the tape with 'Jealous Guy'. Before doubts about sending it to her got the better of me, I packaged up the tape and dropped it into the nearest mailbox.

I felt the slightest tug of guilt as I said good-bye to Bob at the bus depot. I was so nervous that I only vaguely recall the trip westward to Vancouver except that we drove through rain which increased in intensity with each mile. After a flurry of baggage retrieval and taxi hailing, I got to Vancouver International Airport, sopping wet. There I found my sister, looking daisy fresh and ready to take on the world. Once we were airborne, Korinn remarked that my mood seemed to match the wet, gloomy weather. Wasn't I glad to be finally on our way? But I just couldn't seem to shake my apprehension. 'What if Mere isn't the right place? What if there were no St. James or Barons there?'

For Korinn's sake as much as mine, I shook myself out of my funk and made the most of the flight.

As I glanced at Korinn, who was absorbed in an in-flight shopping magazine, I wished I could be more like her. Never worrying about troubles before they happened and only seeing the positive side of life, she had a calming effect on her friends and family.

Many hours later, we dragged ourselves wearily through the interminable customs procession. For the tenth time since we had started our descent to Heathrow, Korinn giggled. "I just can't believe that we are in England."

I echoed her excitement but for different reasons. Despite my restlessness to seek my past, with Mere only days away, I put matters into perspective and concentrated on the first leg of our trip, London.

The next day, reassured by the claim that we could not get lost on the Tube, we ventured forth and were soon awed by this fabulous city. We were thrilled by the changing of the Buckingham Palace guards, shuddered in the infamous Tower of London and revelled at the night lights of Piccadilly Circus and Trafalgar Square. I wrote postcards home, knowing Bob would have loved London.

At last it was time to leave London and catch a morning train for Salisbury. Blue sky and warm air greeted us as we arrived and registered at the Victorian White Horse Hotel with it's charming white lace curtains and window boxes overflowing with vibrantly colored flowers.

Our bags were scarcely deposited in our room when I was on my way to the Tourist Information Centre. I lost no time in asking the young woman there questions about Mere.

"Mere? Why would you want to go there? There's so much to see right here in Salisbury; we have our Cathedral, which has the tallest spire in England; we have Old Sarum, the original part of Salisbury . . . "

Patiently, I broke through her tourist promotion and indicated that I was wanting to get to Mere for family research and asked her for a bus schedule.

In response, she told me that there was but one bus a week to Mere, leaving on Tuesdays and returning to Salisbury on Fridays.

"But I'll be flying home before Tuesday," I said incredulously.

The young woman shrugged as if to dismiss me. Then she recalled a woman who did tours for the Centre and who would be at the White Hart Hotel at 4:00 in the afternoon to arrange the next day's tour. Perhaps we could make arrangements with her.

I contained my frustration with the travel problem until I found Korinn outside basking in the sunshine. Her predictable response was to point out the half timbered public house, advertising fresh scones topped with strawberries and thick Devon cream.

"What if I can't get to Mere? . . . Maybe, I'll have to get a cab . . . I wonder how much that would cost? . . . It's over twenty miles from here."

Over strawberries and cream, Korinn suggested that we go and see the tour lady first. She kept me on an even keel until we headed to the White Hart Hotel.

In the miniature garden behind the Tudor hotel, we joined a lively group of people clustered around a woman who was explaining how she conducted tours by trying to include everyone's request within the area of the map she displayed. I added my request to visit Mere.

"Mere...no one has asked me to go there before, but we should be able to fit it in."

The next morning, replete with a genuine English breakfast, we boarded a rugged looking van and headed out on to the green Salisbury Plain toward Stonehenge. Four other women accompanied us on our journey.

When we arrived at the Druid monument, the air was still and mysterious. I stood in awe at the ancient grey stones that loomed before us. For several seconds, time froze. A warm flow of energy embraced me, leaving me breathless. Just as abruptly the feeling was gone, leaving me with the mystical rings of stone. The presence had been so close; so personal.

Our guide announced our next stop to be Stourhead Gardens. Since Mere was close by, we would drop the others off there, and then she'd drive Korinn and me on to Mere. Between her commentaries about the country through which we travelled, I was fascinated by her statement about her own family roots being traceable to earliest English history.

Beyond Stourhead, the road narrowed and wound its way between miles of hedge-rows bordering rolling green fields. We rounded a corner and without warning, we were in the village of Mere.

Stopping the van in a tiny square our courier pointed out the tourist information office. "The chap who works there will be helpful...I suggest you talk to him...I'll be back to pick you up in about an hour."

Our guide was about to leave when she saw me staring at an enormous grass covered mountain that stood a few meters off in the distance. To my unasked question she said, "That is what was once called the Castle of Mere. A fortress built, I think in the 1200s, maybe earlier."

With that, she drove off leaving me numb with the realization that I had come all this way, only to have a single hour. All I was able to do was look briefly at the enormous green hill, Castlemere. There was no time to do more than that.

I was about to succumb to hysterics because of the short amount of time when Korinn said, "We have a whole hour, let's make the most of it."

At the tiny tourist office we found a big burly red headed man who greeted us pleasantly. At my explanation of doing family research, he offered to help if he could. To my first question concerning St. James families in Mere, his response was negative. To Baron, he offered that a Baron family had lived in Mere for the last few hundred years.

"I suggest you see the Vicar . . . he can tell you more. Here, I'll show you where he lives."

He strode out of the little office with us in his wake. He pointed up a tiny cobblestone lane, indicating a residence near the Parish Church.

As I tried to absorb my surroundings, I contained my excitement of the news of Barons having lived here.

Korinn must have read my mind for as we left the tiny square she began shooting off a roll of film.

The whole village seemed to be a sea of stone. Stone of different types and different shades. Surrounding the square was a radius of small shops, a library and a museum. I soon learned that I had chosen a mid-week closing day and I realized how totally unprepared I was. I hadn't researched properly and here I was paying the price. So, not only did I mess up on finding out about proper transportation, I also picked a day when not even the museum was open. I had just assumed everything would fall into place with a few precise questions. Now, I had to face facts; I had less than one hour to find a family who may have lived here five hundred years ago. I could have laughed or burst into tears. I had no time for either.

Bees humming seemed to be the only sign of life as we walked quickly past stone cottages. A heavy scent of roses assailed us as I rapped on the heavy oak door of the vicarage.

A pleasant middle aged woman greeted us with the information that the Vicar was out. Would we like to come in and wait for his return?

Barely able to contain my impatience, I explained that our time was limited, that I was doing a family history and that I needed to visit the cemetery. She pointed the way along a short lane bordered by a stone wall creeping with roses.

We couldn't find the gate. Time was ticking away. Laughing and shrieking, we clamoured over the rock wall, tumbling to the other side. A light wind blew across the field of headstones as I began searching for a stone bearing the Baron name. There seemed to be no monument dated prior to 1800. Just as I was about to ask help from an elderly caretaker, I saw a tall, thin man approaching us across the cemetery. Pushing his long dark hair from his eyes, the middle aged man breathlessly introduced himself as the Vicar as he expressed his eagerness to be of assistance. Conscious of the rapidly evaporating time, I stole a look at my watch and hurriedly repeated the object of my visit.

"Yes, I am familiar with the Baron name. Come to the church . . . I will show you something interesting."

The Vicar pointed to a stone church standing in the distance. Despite the beautiful blue sky and the hedges of roses gently swaying in the warm breezy air, the church seemed to loom moodily in the distance like a creation from a Bronte novel.

Korinn and I smiled at one another as we left with the Vicar, this time through the gate, toward St. Michael's Church.

We could barely breathe the cold, damp air as we entered the venerable stone building. Pointing to black flagstones on the floor of the church, the Vicar pointed out one inscribed: "John Baron, son of Randolfe Baron, died 1718."

I felt weak as I stared at the name John Baron etched in the dark stone, but realized the date was too recent. As I absorbed this, Korinn snapped a photo of the flagstone.

While the friendly Vicar told of ancient records he had in his house of other Barons, I had to decline his offer to examine them. I had been defeated by the clock. I requested his address; I would be in contact from Canada.

To my unexpressed question he added that Barons were also his ancestors, thus accounting for having this information so readily at hand.

His ancestors were also Barons? That was a coincidence!

"I must confess, Vicar, that I hadn't thought I would find any Barons here so easily . . . the 1400s was such a long time ago."

"1400s?" Distress and some confusion were at once evident in his voice. "I am dreadfully sorry but I just assumed that you meant a more recent period. There are no references to Barons in Mere before the 17th century."

I do not recall our return trip to the hotel room that afternoon. I suddenly just wanted to go home, to have Bob hold me and tell me everything would be all right. But I was not home; Bob was not near, so for Korinn's sake, I carried on with our trip itinerary.

We saw more sights, toured a crumbling castle, and then found ourselves on a speeding train to Heathrow and the flight home. I nearly cried for joy when I passed through Customs and saw "Welcome to Canada" and Bob waiting beyond the barricade.

For the next five days, I stayed in bed, complaining of jet lag but knowing what I was experiencing was a severe let-down. I had been a fool through and through and I was going to have to live with that. Finally, fighting off my mental lethargy, I roused myself and undertook getting back to the routine. Sorting through the accumulation of bills and sales promotions, I came across a bulky envelope bearing American postage. Konni had responded to my taped letter with one of her own.

"Hi, Jewelle . . . I'll save the small talk for later . . . I listened to your story . . . how Mom saw you in another life with John Lennon, who was John Baron, in Castlemere, in the 1400s . . . some of the information wasn't quite right. I guess you're wondering why I say this so I'll explain. Over the last few years as my M.S. has gotten worse, I also seem to have developed psychic abilities. I'll take the liberty of telling you what I see. I see you with a man, a John Baron. But it was in the 1600s, not the 1400s, and not in Castlemere but a place with a name something like 'Penhurst' or 'Petworth' . . . in England. There is a hospital connected to where you lived – maybe involving you directly, I don't know. Oh, one more thing! When I played the song, 'Jealous Guy', I was aware of chimes; not in the song itself . . . but in the background of where you had lived . . ."

Had I heard Konni correctly? I replayed the tape several times before I realized that I had.

# Ten

I was so overwhelmed that I scarcely absorbed the remainder of what Konni had to say. My lethargy lifted; my regret about time and energy wasted sloughed off. Now with this fresh opening; I forgot how my quest had crumbled in Mere. I forgot the tears shed in frustration. All I saw was new hope; hope that I would find Katherine and John after all.

Too excited and impatient to attempt a letter to Konni, I re-wound the tape and in a few curt sentences, asked her to send me absolutely everything she could "see". In the meantime I would be checking on the places she had given me.

I drove to the post office and was paying for special delivery when I felt a tap on my shoulder. "Must be a pretty important letter," observed Debbie quizzically. "How was your trip? I want to hear every detail."

I agreed to her suggestion of going for coffee so long as we did not take too long, explaining to her my need to get to the library to find micro-fiche references. Then I realized how rude I was. I hadn't even called her when I arrived home from England and now I was giving her the brush off.

As soon as the waitress had placed steaming cups of brew before us Debbie's "Well?" demanded some kind of description of my trip.

Hesitantly, I told her that it really was not a success, although as tourists we had a good time. I had not found a St. James in the village of Mere. I told her I did find Barons, even a John Baron, but it was the wrong time period so even finding a Baron, especially a John Baron, was a cruel coincidence. Anyway, the gist of it was, I didn't find my John and Katherine from Mere in the 1400's.

Although I assumed Debbie's expression of regret was mechanical, I felt compelled to tell her about Konni's taped message saying that I had lived in England and had known a John Baron but at a place and a time different from those my mother had given me.

"So now your sister may be right, when your mother wasn't?" asked Debbie, unsuccessfully hiding a smirk.

I was attempting to point out that I did not yet know that my mother had been wrong, when she broke in with, "Jesus, Jewelle, why don't you drop it? What does it matter anyway?"

'What does it matter!' How could she ask that? I didn't know whether to scream or burst into tears. As my friend, I had hoped Debbie understood me. But when I thought about it for a minute, I saw that maybe I was being too hard on her . . . expecting too much from her. What would I have thought if this had been her searching for a past life and paying less attention to this life? Of course, I would wonder . . . so why wouldn't she? I was running out of mental energy to analyze this any longer. All I was certain of was as long as there was a shred of a possibility that Katherine and John had existed, I would have to carry on searching no matter what the price.

Looking at my watch and mumbling something about having to go, I tossed some coins on to the table and bolted out the cafe door.

On my way to spend an hour with genealogy, I passed the librarian and found myself wondering what thoughts about my search lay beyond her friendly smile. I went to the English gazetteer to look for Konni's 'Penhurst' or 'Petworth'. I found a Penhurst, then a Petworth in Sussex. I inserted the Sussex fiche into the reader but neither St. James nor Barons were in either Penhurst or Petworth. Feeling that I was back where I had been when I left Mere, I was just about to leave for home when the librarian intercepted me by holding out a book which had just been catalogued. It was a type of illustrated atlas of England which included brief texts about most of the places, small and large. Politely, I agreed to have a look at the volume. Balancing purse, research papers and the new book precariously on the narrow counter, I flippped through the big shiny pages toPetworth. " . . . Thompson's Hospital built in 1624," I read with surprise.

But unless I could find St. James or Baron families living there what would the mention of a hospital matter?

That night I told Bob of the information from Konni. Shaking his head, he said, "Here we go again, eh?"

"What's that supposed to mean?"

"I'd hoped this trip had gotten this whole thing out of your system. Damn it! How long is this past-life-England- Lennon stuff going to go on?"

I couldn't answer. How in Hell did I know how long it would go on? 'For as long as it takes,' I thought, but not having the nerve to tell him that. Tucking the children into bed, I felt reflective and isolated as I mentally replayed conversations with Konni, Debbie and Bob.

What was the matter with me? I thought of John Lennon, or was it John Baron, every day. It wasn't a rock star that I constantly thought of but a memory of someone familiar. But was this normal? Of course not. Was I going crazy? If I was, why hadn't anybody noticed? Or was I just a very clever crazy person?

I could feel this man John Baron. Was he connected to John Lennon, WAS he John Lennon · 'God damn it,' I would scream to myself · 'Who are you? Where are you?' The only feelings of peace were when I thought simply of a John and Katherine, innocent young people, living so long ago, oblivious to future lives, oblivious to past lives, simply living in England; quiet, green England. These feelings were usually short-lived and again I would agonize as to what the truth really was.

Two days later Konni phoned.

"Why are you phoning in the middle of the day?" I asked. "Did you get my tape? Is something wrong? I found both Penhurst and Petworth but there are no St. James or Barons anywhere."

When she got a word in, Konni told me that if I would be quiet for a minute, she would start at the beginning. That morning she had talked with John Baron.

"What! Did you say you *Talked* to him?"

"... Well, it was not like you and I are talking ... more like images."

Konni went on to recount what she had been 'told' about our past lives together in England in the 1600s. John Baron had come to live with his grandfather in a neighboring town. Your (Katherine's) last name was *James*, not St. James. You were to have been married but he sickened and died. I saw you as a nurse. I don't know if you were actually nursing him but I did see you in a hospital. He had a cart or was taken away in a cart. You wore a blue dress when you worked at the hospital ... the hospital wasn't like a modern one at all ... it just had a big room or hall. His death was such a trauma that it has affected both of you in all of your lives since then.

She explained that pain eventually surfaces in many different ways. "For Lennon, or Baron, it was in his music; for you it was in the grief you felt when he died. While you had never paid him any attention as a Beatle, with the sudden manner of his death, you were shocked into allowing emotions, suppressed for many lifetimes to surface. It was this sudden and traumatic death in this past life that you still need to deal with. If you could remember the Katherine-John story, you could work this past grief out and carry on."

After hearing this I was sobbing my heart out to my sister, by long distance from California. "It's so hard ... I get so lonely ... I can't talk to people about this ... it sounds so weird ... and do you know what's so bloody frustrating? That he had to be *John Lennon* ... a rock star! The one I loved and lost was just 'John'."

But was John Baron really John Lennon? Or did Lennon represent a sudden loss; a loss of someone who was loved; loved by so many? Did his death simply symbolize my own losses; loss of youth, loss of Patrick, loss of dreams? Little did I know that this question would never be fully answered, but answered just enough to keep me asking.

47

I was beginning to tire. I knew I had to check out Konni's new information of Katherine's name being "James", *not* "St. James". Back at the library, my hopes weren't very high as I half-heartedly inserted the Sussex fiche into the reader.

Slowly turning the wheel to James, I didn't know whether to laugh or scream... there was Katherine James... in fact there were *two* of them! Born ten years apart! Both in Petworth! Was I one of them? I nearly turned away in total frustration. For years, I couldn't find one Katherine and now I had to figure out which Katherine was which. Forcing myself to be calm, I remembered what my mother had said so long ago. "Katherine's father was named Robert."

Examining the two "Katherines", I first saw "Katherine James, daughter of William born in 1656, Petworth, Sussex." Then I saw it... there it was! "Katherin James, daughter of Robert James, christened February 24, 1666, Petworth, Sussex."

(While I assumed I would have been the one with the father named Robert, I wanted to get more information. So I later wrote to the Records Office for Sussex and received this letter... "There were several James families in Petworth in the mid 17th century. From the index of Petworth Marriages and Baptisms, it seems there are at least three Katherine James in Petworth at that period. One was the wife of William James, one the daughter of William James and one the daughter of Robert James. The variation in the spelling of the entries signifies nothing at all, since spelling was not standardized at all, and the same person's name was often spelled in several different ways.")

I had to see the entry again. Once more my attention was on the Sussex fiche. As I stared, my heart thumped. 'Just imagine... I'm looking at my birth record from three hundred years ago...'

Katherine James, christened February 24, 1666, Petworth, Sussex, father Robert James.

Suddenly, I could remember the village of Petworth in the seventeenth century. I could see it in much the same way as I could remember my childhood home in my present life.

I could visualize the narrow crooked lanes swelled with mud in spring, the stench of open sewers in summer, the beautiful

48

scarlet vines enshrouding stone cottages in autumn. I felt Katherine's presence. She and I were the same soul. I rushed home, gathering pens and paper. I had to try and capture these memories for myself on paper. As I began to write, my words were at first hesitant and slow. I had never written a story nor did I have a vivid imagination. However, memories from somewhere flooded me as the story unfolded effortlessly. I began to scribble . . . Year 1682 . . .

# Eleven

## Katherine's Story

Robert James watched the slow moving lines of seamen emerging from the ships with barrels hoisted over their shoulders. It was the King's Fleet, but he liked to think of it as his since he controlled the goods when they were unloaded. Chichester Harbour was a scurry with lesser merchants waiting anxiously for barrels of sugar, silks, oranges and spices.

As they picked up their goods on the dock, Robert counted, sorted and collected gold coin from the trade merchants who were about to travel to London. There it would filter through the country, everyone adding a coin here and pence there.

Wives and whores stood together on the docks to see their men after months at sea. Children ran about the docks laughing and shouting. Dogs barked; there was excitement in the air. After months of cold grey foggy days, sparsely laid tables and little dance, the sun shone again as spring and the ships arrived together.

Tonight there would be wine flowing, dancing and full bellies for even the street urchins who would soon be curled up by a tavern fire, not seen by the merry makers around them.

Robert drank a mug of dark smooth ale but kept his head clear and his gold close, for his business was not yet over. The next few days would be played over and over again for him, counting gold and over-seeing the distribution of goods. He could then leave for home in Petworth and feel satisfied.

Katherine sat by the fire with her two younger sisters, indulging their childish chatter.

"Tell us about Maggie Hatchett's father," Elizabeth said, "Maggie says if he doesn't get well again, she and her mama could end up in the poorhouse."

Mary asked in her baby voice, "Katie, what's a poor- house?"

Elizabeth, ignoring Mary, said "Maggie says her father makes noises that scare her . . . gurgling and choking."

Mary tugged at Katherine's sleeve, "Katie, Lizzie says you empty chamber-pots at the hospital, just like Polly does here . . . is that true, Katie?"

Their mother had entered the room quietly and could not hide her disapproval. "Young ladies should not talk so, and about chamber-pots. Katherine does a service to her family by helping the sick, the poor and the homeless. She will learn humility and gratitude for her station to be with those less fortunate."

Her speech had been heard many times by them all. They hid their smiles and did not look at one another.

"Mother, when will father be home from Chichester?" Katherine asked. Not that she was interested so much in her father's return but in changing the subject.

"When the ships are in his business just begins. You should not need to ask; he has done this all sixteen years of your life."

*Although I could remember my life as Katherine, I was having trouble recalling her family clearly. (Months after the story had been written I checked on micro-fiche to see if Katherine had had these sisters, Mary and Elizabeth. Mary did not exist but Katherine did have a younger sister, Elizabeth, christened in December 1670.) For Katherine's parents I had a feeling of respect and fear, but I couldn't imagine a feeling of love. I could remember a servant or more like a nanny, a warm woman . . . I wondered, where was she now?*

Polly, their old and dear servant, entered the room announcing their night meal was ready. Mother and three daughters ate a small meal of pork pie and wine, then retired to bed.

Mother came to Katherine's bed-chamber as she often did when her father was away.

"Katherine, this year on May Day you will be attending the ball at the Great Hall. I remember when I was young, there was not as much dancing and merry making... the youth of today have it so much easier," she mused to herself more than to her daughter, who was thinking more of the morrow tending the sick and poor Mister Hatchett.

Katherine awoke to the patter of rain. Polly brought to her room some cider with bread and cheese. "Here you are, Miss, and you best wear your cloak. The rain is cold even though 'tis spring," she fussed.

As Katherine left the grey stone house, she went through their small garden to the lane. Yesterday, the flowers were opening and the stone bench was warm and inviting. Today, it was cold and wet but she still felt it was beautiful. The rain was heavier now. She had a mile to walk through the small narrow lanes to the hospital. She tried unsuccessfully to avoid the puddles, for when the cobblestones ended the Sussex mud began.

She walked head down, only seeing the front of her leather shoes fighting battle with the mud. She didn't see the cart or driver until she heard, "My lady, what do I find in the rain?"

She slowly raised her eyes and looked into the bluest eyes that Katherine, in her small world, had ever seen.

"Lady, may I give you shelter and accompany you to your destination?"

She stood there awkwardly; she had never seen this stranger before on the small lanes of Petworth. He had an air of someone who had seen much more of the world than she.

"Miss?" he asked questioningly.

Wondering if he mocked her, she answered, "Why thank you, Sire," and as he offered his hand, she gave him hers and into the cart she went.

Now that she was sitting beside him she felt foolish, and sat there staring at him. His face was handsome but not pretty, his hair was the color of sand, but it was his eyes that held her attention.

"May I introduce myself?" As he smiled his eyes also smiled. "I am John Baron. I come from Fittleworth where I have recently come to live with my grandfather. I have to show my Grandfather Baron that I am worthy enough to be sent to school in Oxford at his expense. He does not part easily with his coffers or his favour and does not believe men should spend time on books in Latin, when there are such things as trade, hunting, and more manly past-times to be learned. But, I am his namesake and for that reason he will indulge me, if I can prove myself worthy." He laughed suddenly, "My lady, I have been prattling on like a fool and I know not where to escort you."

*I could see this blue eyed, sandy headed man as vividly as if I had seen him only yesterday. Someone I had lost track of . . . but someone I had known very well.*

"To the hospital."

"Are you ill, my lady?"

"Nay, I too have worthiness to show. By offering my services to the sick, poor and homeless, I will learn humility and be grateful for my station in life."

"You say those words like you have heard them many times."

"Yes," she laughed, "many times."

As they neared the hospital, the sun broke through the grey clouds. John looked up and said, "I'm sure 'tis the same warmth that you bring those wretches in there, when you arrive at their bedside . . . a light on a cloudy day."

Katherine felt suddenly warm and she was not sure if it was the sun or this stranger that made her feel this way. Suddenly she jumped down from the cart. "Gads, I must hurry." She realized she had tarried too long and was sure the Matron Agnes would be waiting. She gave a small curtsey while saying, "Good bye, Sir Baron."

Now it was his turn to stare. He watched her slight but strong figure scurry away. Katherine's hair fell across her back, thick and dark, bouncing as she ran.

As expected, Matron Agnes was at the other end of the massive hallway, but Katherine could feel her scowl from a distance.

"Miss Katherine James," the matron's voice cut through the air like a chill in winter. "If you are to do service to this hospital, you will arrive before the hour of eight, not any later."

"Yes, mistress," she mumbled. "The mud made it very slow walking this morn."

She could see Agnes was not convinced, so she hurried off to begin her duties before the matron could say more. And as Katherine hurried along, she thought of the man with the smiling blue eyes.

*I felt uneasy when I wrote of the matron Agnes. I couldn't visualize her features but her presence made me extremely uncomfortable. I again began to question my sanity as these people from Petworth were becoming real human beings to me. I feared Agnes; I was fond of Mister Hatchett; our servant, Polly, made me feel warm and loved.*

"Good morn, Mister Hatchett," Katherine smiled at the dying man as she noticed his color was not so sallow today.

"Ah, my child, I pray to sweet Jesus, that these old bones carry me not through another winter."

Katherine tried to look shocked, "Dear Mister Hatchett, you will be back to the docks by the end of summer, fit again with the sea breeze in your face. Now no more talk of dying."

"Yes, but . . . ," he was interrupted by a violent coughing and wheezing. As Katherine wiped the drool off his face, she felt fortunate to be sixteen years of age and not to worry of death; but to feel good that it was spring.

The day went on as every other. In the morning the patients in her care were fed some bread soaked in milk. Their hands and feet were washed and she tucked their coverlets around them as Polly would Elizabeth and Mary. She tended the fires and found time to gossip with Jane, who was doing service time as she was. Prayers were read to the patients twice a day, although Katherine wondered if anyone was listening; for if God was, she had never seen a sign; but such thoughts she never voiced.

When the day was done and the night watchers arrived,

Katherine left with Jane as they walked through the narrow lanes to their homes. They parted halfway through the village, each going her own direction. As Katherine arrived at the garden gate she took time to sit for a moment on the stone bench, thinking of the man from Fittleworth. This morning seemed so long away.

*At the time of writing this I had no idea what night watchers were, I thought I was simply inventing the word. Years later I learned that night watchers were at institutions where the patients had the plague or other infectious diseases. The night watchers were to assure that no one escape the hospital, thus preventing further spread of dread diseases.*

A week passed with no break in routine except for a free day on Sunday. This day Katherine spent with her family. In the morning they walked to their parish church for services. Elizabeth fidgeted while Mary fell asleep and Mother pretended not to notice, but this was all routine. In the afternoon Katherine sat in the garden doing embroidery while the girls chattered steadily. That evening as they were about to sup, carriages were heard. Elizabeth shrieked with delight, "Father's home. Father's home!"

They all rushed to the hall to greet Robert James, who carried delightful looking boxes and packages. He had gifts for everyone; laces and bows for the younger girls; her mother was pleased with a new fashionable muff and exotic perfume.

Katherine waited patiently and was soon rewarded. A bundle of silk emerged from a carefully wrapped sack. Rich, dark green enveloped her, as her mother wrapped the fabric around her shoulders, giving a look of approval to her husband. "Polly will have this made into a fine gown in time for the May Day Ball."

"Thank you, Mother ... and Father," she breathed. She knew at sixteen years, she would attend the ball but she had no idea she would have a fine new gown. Now she looked forward to this day immensely. Two weeks seemed a long time to wait.

*I seemed to be losing touch with my present surroundings. Physically I took care of my family but my mind had become Katherine's mind. My stomach fluttered in anticipation of the upcoming ball that Katherine would attend ... or was it Jewelle*

*attending? Insomnia became a problem and when I did sleep,
I dreamed of Katherine and John dancing ... always dancing.*

The days passed slowly. Katherine longed to be outside in the sun and fresh air to pick flowers and watch the baby lambs in the fields. The poor souls in the hospital; some lay in their beds listlessly; some were demanding and cranky; and some were ready to enter the next world. Mister Hatchett did not talk anymore though he did smile occasionally, and as Katherine cooled a fevered brow or brought flowers to a woman whose days were nearly over, she saw the laughing blue eyes and wondered if John Baron had only been a dream.

May Day arrived. Excitement had been building all week. Older children had been practising the Maypole dance. Booths were set up throughout the square in the center of the village with food and drink for sale. A fortune teller was there but lest she be a witch, only the brave neared her. A tooth extractor was there for the entertainment of those who could stomach such scenes; it was not entertaining for the poor wretches with fat cheeks. Men of labour became knights for the day and some were even injured because of their lack of jousting knowledge. Village girls made eyes at young farm boys, who equally made eyes back.

Katherine arrived as usual at the hospital and until noon, routine was kept. As she and Jane ate their noon-day meal of meat pies, Agnes approached them and sternly clipped, "If the fires are stoked well and the patients are tended to, you may leave for the day. As tomorrow is the Sabbath, I will not expect you till Monday morn."

"Thank you, Mistress," they solemnly replied in unison.

Agnes bowed her head slightly and left them to continue their meal.

When she had left, they started to giggle as Katherine whispered, "Maybe she has a heart after all."

Jane laughed, "But I wouldn't want to say a prayer on it. We best hurry before her mood changes."

Within an hour they were gone.

Katherine hurried home to change out of her plain hospital

shift and into a muslin frock. She roamed the square and found her sisters pulling Polly this way and that. Polly was glad to see her.

"Oh, Lady Katherine, I finished your gown this morn... do be home in time to bathe...and, oh, we must arrange your hair," she went on fussing.

Elizabeth and Mary were tired but happy as they followed the swish of Polly's skirts all the way home. As Katherine followed them, she remembered being a small girl and the joy of May Day.

Now it was the joy of the night she anticipated. The knot in the pit of her stomach grew by the hour. Even though she was excited, she did not know what to expect. "But soon enough I will," she thought.

"Go wait in your chamber, my lady, and I will draw you a bath," Polly ordered, still fussing.

The metal tub which was used for special occasions, was now filled with steamy water with lavender scents thrown in. Katherine quickly undressed and let the warmth envelope her body. She felt calmer now and was anxious to see how her new gown would enhance her, or make her look like Lizzie playing in her mother's gowns.

Polly rubbed her skin with a rough cloth until it tingled. Over a small shift she slipped on the gown. It was plain rich green with a rounded neck and sleeves that puffed to her elbow and flowed gently from her waist. Polly then brushed her hair until it shone, weaving a string of tiny pearls through the locks which cascaded down her back.

"M'lady, you are beautiful," sighed Polly.

Katherine was afraid to look in the glass but as she peeked she felt pleased and yes, she did look beautiful. She stood there for a minute enjoying the feel of the silk on her skin. A knock came on the door.

"Mother!" Katherine was surprised and gasped when she saw what her mother was holding.

"These are for you, my sweet," said that proud woman, as she lovingly fastened an emerald choker around her daughter's neck. "It was your Grandmother James...the day you were born, she bequeathed it, to be given to you on a special day in your sixteenth year."

Unaccustomed to this show of affection, Katherine felt embarrassed, when her mother abruptly announced, "Your father is waiting . . . it is time to be on our way."

As they entered the Great Hall, they were announced by the Grand Marshall (who on every other day was known as Willie the town crier.) Tonight was different, however, and his voice sang out . . . "Master Robert James, Mistress Anne James and Miss Katherine James."

They walked through a flowered archway and were greeted briefly by the Petworth mayor. It all happened so quickly and they were soon mingling in the crowd while the other guests were being announced. She recognized nearly everyone as friends of her father's and also their neighbors. The room was quite full now. Amongst the ladies there was a small hum of chatter and gossip. The smell of perfume filled the air. The ladies admired each other's gowns while each secretly thought hers was the finest. The gentlemen were in green or navy tunics and wore leather shoes with shiny buckles.

Katherine was gazing at the wonder of it all when she heard the Grand Marshall announce, "John Baron of Fittleworth."

*I could smell the perfume in the air and hear the steady hum of chatter as the great hall became increasingly full. There was excitement in the air. I seemed to stand as a spectator viewing the festive scene before me. The memory came as easily as if I had only just attended the ball yesterday. When I would pause from the writing, looking at my modern surroundings, I felt so very sad.*

Katherine could feel the hard and steady thumping of her heart and as John made his greeting to the mayor, she took in every detail of his being. His light blue shirt with ruffles accented the rich blue velvet tunic. His knee length pants were met by black leather boots. His sandy hair fell across his forehead but it was again his eyes that held her attention. They were clear and steady as they gazed about the room. She hoped he would see her, and then felt foolish, for even if he did, there was no way to catch his eye with so many lovely ladies in the room.

Robert Philp, tall and gangly, was in front of her asking her to be his partner in a new court jig. He and Katherine had known each other since childhood.

"I'm sorry, Robert, not just yet... I would like to watch the dancing... I may not be able to perform properly..." she trailed off.

*I could see Robert's red face as clearly as the words on this page. I didn't want to hurt him. He was a friend but I just couldn't dance with him. Strange as this sounds, three hundred years later, I still feel guilty for the hurt I saw in his eyes.*

Her mother, who was standing beside her, whispered sharply, "Katherine."

"I'm sorry, Robert," pretending not to hear her mother.

Robert was red faced and flustered but bowed quickly and went in pursuit elsewhere. Her mother looked sharply at her again.

Then Katherine saw John coming across the room. She had not seen him watching her. He, too, had taken in every detail from her rich green gown, to her thick, shiny hair. He was standing before her and she had not noticed before how very tall he was. As John looked down into her eyes, he smiled and asked, "Is this the same girl I found in the rain?"

She smiled, feeling shy, as warmth crept into her face. Her mother was watching and questioned, "Katherine?"

"Ah, Mother... Father... this is John Baron who resides with his grandfather in Fittleworth. Master Baron rescued me from the rain and mud one day on my route to the hospital."

"I see," her mother replied, but Katherine was not sure what her mother saw.

Her father bowed slightly and said nothing but Katherine recognized the piercing, watchful look in his eyes.

The fiddlers struck up a new melody; John turned to Katherine's mother and father saying, "Excuse us, Madame... Sir," as he offered Katherine his arm.

She laid her hand gingerly on his sleeve as he led her to the dance floor. As they danced, all she was aware of was the warmth of his body and the firmness of his hands in hers.

"I have missed you, little one. I longed to seek you out but my

Grandfather insists that before I think of life's pleasures, I must first learn some lessons of life."

As they danced, they would gaze at one another solemnly and then would laugh at nothing. Katherine had never felt so happy or so safe.

*I could see the ballroom as clearly as if I were dancing there right now. The hall was decorated with flowers, the air was warm, everyone was happy, or did they seem to be reflecting my happiness? If I could choose a frozen space in time to live, this is where I would dwell forever. Bob called out to me, asking about dinner. I burst into tears.*

The hall was becoming hot from the dancing and the excitement in the air. John whispered, "Pray, let us escape for a short while."

Katherine followed him through the flowered archway outside to the stone terrace as the cool air caressed their faces. They fell silent as they strolled along the stones. The sky was clear; bright stars shared the night with them. The moon was at it's fullest so lanterns were not needed.

"Did you know, my lady, that I am a scholar of the stars?"

He then looked up to the sky and said, "'Tis fate that I met you in the rain, my lady ... see ... 'tis written in the stars."

Before she could answer he put his hands under her chin and kissed her, first softly and then more intensely. He was more surprised than she. Katherine had never known such closeness. Surely, he had known many young ladies? Why did he express such feelings of tenderness for her? She longed for him to sweep her up in his arms and keep her there, to protect her from the world forever.

Katherine sat in her bed-chamber gazing out the small window. She was back home in body, but her spirit was still dancing the night away. Why, I am in love, she laughed at herself for that self-realization. Sleep did not come easily that night.

Polly was shaking her. "Miss Katherine, wake up, wake up ... there is a young man asking for you. He is waiting in the garden."

"Please tell Mother that I am ill and will not be attending church . . . oh, please, Polly," Katherine begged.

Polly started to say something, but a look on the girl's face stopped her. "Oh, very well, run along," she said.

She threw on a light summer dress and wrapped a shawl across her shoulders. John sat on the stone bench with his long legs stretched out lazily in front of him. When he saw her, he jumped up, making a mock bow, "Your carriage awaits my lady."

She laughed, "Where do we go, dear sir?"

"Ah, you shall see . . . I have brought bread and cheese, fruit and ale, so we may never again return." And as he helped her into the cart, she laughed again.

They drove through the lanes that went this way and that, past the hospital, then over the little stone bridge into the country. The grass in the fields was green with new spring growth and wild flowers were everywhere. And as the morning sun began to warm them, Katherine marveled at how beautiful the world was.

They stopped beside a small river and as John unhitched the horse to let him drink and eat freely, Katherine spread a rug and laid out their meal. After they ate, they walked barefoot in some tall grass and when Katherine shrieked at a small snake, John roared with laughter, picked her up in his arms and said, "I will always save you from life's many evils."

His laughter must have been too much for him, for he lost his breath and started coughing and choking. Katherine thumped him gently on his back and when the color returned to his face she retorted, "'Tis your own fault for laughing at me. You are a lucky man that I was here to save you from yourself."

Monday morning arrived dull and grey. Polly brought her breakfast as usual and as Katherine ate, the old servant searched her face but Polly was to be disappointed. The girl offered no account of the day before. As Katherine walked to work her step was light.

As she entered the hallway, Agnes was waiting for her.

"Lady Katherine, take off your cloak promptly and tend to Mister Hatchett. His hours are few and until his family arrives, he'll need someone by his side."

61

Poor, poor man, she thought, as she hurried to his side. His face was grey and his breathing shallow. She took the weathered old hand in hers and crooned to him. "Do not give up, Mister Hatchett. Wait for your wife and wait for Maggie." Did his hand pump hers or was it just twitching? . . . She was not sure. They sat as such for an hour until mercifully his family arrived.

Agnes approached Misses Hatchett and said, "Now, make your peace for he'll not be here by night's fall." The nurses left them alone, for his life was now in God's hands.

They resumed their duties, stoked the fires, washed down the floor of the hall and tried to cheer up the other patients who were well aware that they could be the next to go. The Vicar arrived and shortly after he left, Mister Hatchett also was gone.

Katherine had watched many deaths and often wondered if the pain felt as bad as it looked. She was secretly relieved she did not have to cry and suffer as she had seen so many others do.

Leaving for the day, Katherine felt subdued and quiet. Walking slowly through the lanes, she said a prayer for Mister Hatchett. As she entered the garden, there on the stone bench sat John. Suddenly, she felt like a little girl and rushed to him, putting her hands around his. He chuckled and said, "See, my life is in your hands." Then, seeing her distress asked, "What is it?"

"Oh, 'tis nothing . . ." she sighed and as she looked into his eyes, she was glad all was fine in her world.

The summer was a happy time. Katherine worked steadily at the hospital and when the stench of the hall grew unbearable or when Agnes frowned with some displeasure, she would think of John with his rugged face and sky blue eyes and she would feel happy.

John spent a good part of the summer riding the lush green countryside around Petworth and for his grandfather's approval he became a quick and strong hunter. He also learned the art of the sword but in his heart his joys were with reading, writing, and the study of the stars. Life for John was good and he intended it to stay that way. The nagging chest pain which he got from time to time would go away, he was sure, when his riding and exercise were over.

Autumn was arriving and the days were becoming less bright. Sundays were when John and Katherine could both escape from their duties. It was the first Sunday in October that he arrived in the garden to call on her. "In my riding with Grandfather, I have found a place that you must see."

Katherine was mildly curious but as long as she went with him it did not really matter where they went. This day they started on the road to Chichester. Chichester, however, was not where they were headed. A few miles down the road, John turned the buggy into a narrow path that wandered through a lightly wooded area. He then pulled the reins of the horse and they stopped. She looked at him, raising her eyebrows in question, as he said, "My love, we shall take a walk."

They walked amongst the thin trees and were now walking across what looked like a farmer's field, when all at once the earth came to an end. They were standing on top of a massive set of deep cliffs.

"John," she gasped, "it's beautiful...it's like being on top of England!"

He smiled to see that he had pleased her. "Everyone should have their own place in the world and from this time on, this will be our place."

They stood looking out across the valley with the small rolling hills. The golden face of the cliffs melted into the orange and yellow bushes below. They walked along a windy path on a ridge along the top of the cliffs, laughing and feeling like children on a spring day.

As they went round a corner they nearly collided with a small boy who was skipping and chattering to himself. He was a chubby little thing with long brown curls. John bowed deeply, "Pleased to make your acquaintance, young man."

The boy eyed them suspiciously, then decided to be friendly. He smiled and blurted out, "One day I shall be a knight for the King...the bravest and strongest knight in the land."

Mildly surprised, John smiled at the boy and said, "Yes, I believe you will."

Katherine asked, "What shall we call you, Sir knight?"

63

"Jo-Jo," he replied.

John grabbed a bunch of wildflowers from the ground and with the flowers touched the boy's shoulders, first one side then the other.

"I knight thee Sir Jo-Jo of Sussex."

And away the little boy ran, yelling at invisible foe, with his curls flying behind him.

As they watched the little fellow leave, John said thoughtfully, "We shall name our first child Jo-Jo."

Katherine gulped, "Child, but that would mean . . ."

"Yes, dear Katherine, will you be my wife?"

Katherine felt the world spinning and oh, how she loved the world and how she would love these cliffs forever but more than anything how she loved this man standing there looking down upon her. "Yes, my John," she barely breathed, "I will be your wife."

He smiled and between kissing her lips, whispered sweet nothings in her ear.

Ten days passed since John's proposal and she had not seen him. He had not shown up the following Sunday. Maybe he has changed his mind, she thought wildly, and has gone to Oxford, or, or . . . ? Her mind was a panic.

Over the next week, Katherine worked hard; not out of dedication but as a means of passing time. Another Sunday passed with still no sign of John. She sat in the garden and wept. The air was clear and cold, but the only chill she felt was in her heart.

When she arrived at the hospital on Monday morn, Agnes was waiting as usual with the day's instructions.

"Good morning, Miss James," she greeted her curtly. "We have a new patient this morn. His grandfather brought him to us in the dead of night. He says the young man has been burning with fever for two weeks. He has trouble breathing and has vicious chest pains. What you are to do is apply compresses to his chest, give him plenty to drink and keep his brow cool."

Katherine went first to the kitchen for rags and water, then to find her new patient.

"Sweet Jesus, John!"

There he lay...his hair falling over his brow, in the old familiar way, and when she reached for his hand, it was weak.

"Oh, Katherine, in my dreams I have tried to reach you."

"Shh," she whispered.

"Please make me well, Katherine, for I have a wedding to attend."

"My sweet sire, you will be as new as a spring lamb in May ...all you need is rest."

And as she applied the steamy compresses and looked into his eyes, she tried to believe her own words. She stayed with him late that night, and left for home only when he was sleeping. The next morning she was up before the sun and gone long before Polly brought her morning meal.

Agnes wasn't in the hall when Katherine arrived. She threw off her cloak and went straight to John.

"Good morning, dear Sir," she smiled, then the smile froze on her face. His usually clear eyes were glazed and his face was hot and flushed. She ran for some water, which he drank quickly, then still clutching her hand he fell into a deep sleep.

"Katherine," she heard Agnes call, "What are you doing here so early?" Then not waiting for an answer, she went on ... "no matter...Katherine, the young man you are attending is dying...so try and give him comfort."

"Matron Agnes, what do you mean, this man is dying?" she hissed. "This man only needs rest. He is young and strong...how can you say he is dying?"

"Miss James," Agnes said slowly, trying to control her impatience, "this man is dying...he has consumption...I will not discuss it further, but to give you proper instructions on how best to care for him."

Katherine listened but did not hear. When Agnes finished Katherine slowly walked to the kitchen, her eyes stinging with tears. She felt her whole soul would break into a million pieces. But she knew she *had* to be strong. She poured some broth into a cup and carried it back to the hall. John was watching her.

He saw her red eyes and asked, "What's amiss?"

"'Tis Agnes...we had words...the woman makes my cry in frustration at times...now drink this broth...it will make you feel good, I promise."

The days passed as John grew weaker. The days and nights became as one.

One morning Katherine arrived at grey dawn; she could see John trying to sit up but not having the strength to do so. Gurgling noises rasped at his chest. She put her arm behind his back and slowly sat him up. His uneven breathing slowly returned to normal. Katherine held him as she would a child. Suddenly, he straightened himself up and seemed to possess the strength of the John she once knew. His eyes were piercing as he looked into hers.

"Katherine, I am not a fool...tell me what the Matron says. Am I to be well or will I lie here like an old man, until I shrivel up and die. Curses, Katherine, tell me."

Her eyes swelled up with tears...and there was no need to answer him. John held Katherine to him but what she couldn't see were the blue eyes clouded in tears.

Suddenly, he flung her aside and started ranting, "Katherine, it's not fair, it's not fair. How can you love me? Look at me... I'm a sick cripple."

Jane, who was carrying some broth, came running and tried to calm him down. He swung his arm, sending the tray clattering onto the stone floor. "Leave me be, you wench," he screamed.

Jane backed up, not knowing what to do. Katherine mustered all the strength she had ever possessed.

"John Baron, *stop*! I love you as much today as I did on the first day we met in the rain." Her voice softened, "I'll always love you...forever I'll love you...we'll ride this storm out together."

"Don't you understand," he pleaded. "I can't leave you to face the world alone."

She curled up beside him and whispered, "Of course I understand."

*I tried to leave Petworth and concentrate on my present surroundings but it was no use. I wept as I wrote. I had to go back to John. He was dying. God, don't let him die, I cried, but*

*I knew it was inevitable. I knew I should take a rest from the writing. I'd developed a fever and a deep cough within my chest. Severe pains shot through my stomach.*

*The doorbell rang. Joanne called to me, "Mom, it's Debbie." In a daze I went to the door. "Hi," I said feebly, trying to sound normal . . . but what the hell was normal anyway?*

*"Where have you been hiding?"*

*"I'm writing a story," I mumbled, "about John and Katherine . . . I'll call you when I'm finished."*

*Debbie looked at me with concern which quickly turned to impatience. "Jewelle, you're living in another world. Can't you see this compulsion? You're ruining your life. Can't you understand?"*

But John knew that Katherine really did not understand at all. For a long time after, they lay side by side. Neither said a word. Finally, he slept.

John's life was leaving him day by day. Katherine would sit with him for hours while he drifted in and out of sleep. Late one night he opened his eyes and they were clear.

"Katherine," he said, as he reached for her hand, smiling faintly, "I promise I'll always be with you. Always remember we are a part of each other . . . remember . . . 'tis in the stars."

Katherine sat for a very long time watching him sleep. Exhausted, she too slept. When she awoke, she saw that she would never again see him smile, feel his touch, or gaze into those sky blue eyes. He was gone.

Time stopped. Weeks (or was it months?) later Katherine slowly regained her senses. She woke in strange surroundings. She was in an attic room but where? Only when she peered out a small window, recognizing Aunt Agatha's garden did her memory jog to that cold windy night, when she had been brought here, screaming and kicking, entrusted to Aunt Agatha's care.

Unsteadily, she staggered to the door as a coughing fit wracked her body. The door was locked. She started to scream . . . and scream for Aunt Agatha or the family's maid to let her find John.

Aunt Agatha burst through the door. Her calm voice purred, "Now, now, Katherine, it's time for your medicine."

"I want to see John..."

'Silly girl,' thought Agatha, 'pining over a young man who could have offered her very little.' Agatha knew her brother's family was foolish to let Polly spoil Katherine all these years.

Aunt Agatha hissed, "I've had enough...you know very well your John is gone."

And as she had done for weeks, Katherine swallowed the laudanum. Agatha wondered if she'd given her more than the usual dose. Shrugging her shoulders she left the room, locking the door behind her.

Katherine quickly entered the dream-like state and as she began to drift, she could see John beckoning to her. Then, her tiny body became very still as her soul rushed in ecstasy to join with his.

And at that very moment, Jo-Jo, who played in the fields, thought he heard singing in the sky.

*A week passed while I wrote this story and in those seven days I lived completely in another century. Coming back to my present day life was the hardest reality I've ever faced.*

*I have left Katherine's story in it's original and un-edited form. Some of the facts I was able to check out and others have so far eluded me.*

*However, my feelings and memories of how Katherine felt remain crystal clear.*

*After scrawling the last sentence, I collapsed onto the couch falling into a deep sleep...and as I slept, John and Katherine danced...*

# Twelve

The shrill ring of the telephone awoke me.

"Your story is nearly right on," Konni blurted, all the way from California.

Startled and sleepy, I managed to respond, "My story? How do you know there is a story?"

"Actually, I didn't... but John did."

"John? What John?"

"Baron. He's been watching you write and he said you were pretty close to how it all happened... so, you are doing it, Jewelle!"

"Doing what?"

"Remembering."

I was determined that Bob and Debbie read my story; perhaps it would make them understand. That evening when the children were asleep, I found Bob stretched out on the couch reading that day's paper. Before he knew what happened, I had it out of his hands and substituted it with 'Katherine's Story'. A captive audience, he did not have much choice but to read my literary effort. While he read of Katherine's lost love, I sat watching his face. For years he had watched helplessly and without understanding the anguish which seemed to consume me. The almost patronizing expression on his face gave way to one of empathy as he reached the final pages. He might not have liked it, but he was beginning to grasp, for the first time, something of what I was really about.

The next morning, I ventured a first contact with Petworth – composing a letter of inquiry to the Historical Society of Sussex requesting information on the earlier times in Petworth. I packaged up copies of the story for dispatch to Konni and my mother. In Mother's I enclosed a note saying, "I have found my village at last. Petworth is about fifty miles south of London. It's close to a town called Hastlemere . . . sounds like Castlemere, doesn't it? I found out that Katherine was 'James' not 'St. James', and she was born in 1666. You were right about her father's name being Robert. Konni has been helping me. Why didn't you tell me she is psychic? Or did you know? Both you and Konni were aware of chimes when listening to 'Jealous Guy' . . . interesting eh? Of course, chimes will be hard to check out."

After piling the mail near the door, I dialed Debbie's number and invited myself over. Minutes later, I was at her door and before she had a chance to say anything, I shoved a copy of Katherine's story into her hands, ordering her to read it. I would pick it up the next day and would stay to visit. Then I was out the door and in my car; Debbie had not uttered a word.

Driving home the radio belted out, 'I Saw Her Standing There' and I slipped into a reverie. The ball held in the Great Hall . . . I would not dance with Robert Philp . . . would Robert have actually existed? Was Mister Hatchett real? . . . and John's grandfather? Would their names be on record? In the middle of our quiet residential street, I made a U-turn, heading in the direction of the library.

Within minutes of getting the correct micro-fiche, I rolled up the surname, Philp . . . and there, staring at me was, "Robert Philp, christened 1664, Petworth, Sussex!" Then I found "Hatchett". In my story, Katherine had known her patient only as "Mr. Hatchett". Here was a Henry Hatchett from the right time period.

John, not being from the Petworth area would not appear, but what of his grandfather? In my story, I had written " . . . I am John Baron. I live with my grandfather in Fittleworth . . . I am his namesake." I slowly advanced the reel and there on the screen was: "John Baron married Susan Elson, Fittleworth, Sussex, 1627." I could barely read through my incredulous tears. A shiver ran down my spine. Could this be John's grandfather?

"Well, what do you think?" I asked, as Debbie poured coffee and handed my story back. "Could you picture Katherine's life and how she felt?"

"It is a nice little story... but it's only that, Jewelle, a story. Dammit, I have to level with you. You're living in another world. When you first mentioned this 'past-life' with John Lennon... remember... when we went for lunch in Vancouver? Well, I didn't want to say anything to hurt your feelings but I thought it was all a little far-fetched. I did try and sympathize with you so you wouldn't get upset... but really, Jewelle... think about it. It's ridiculous! I mean he was John Lennon... and you're a housewife from small town British Columbia... when we were young you didn't even care about the Beatles. What is happening to you? I hope you haven't talked to anybody else about this... they just might think you're crazy," Debbie concluded with a giggle.

"Debbie," I said, as evenly as I could, "Katherine James is me ...she existed. I can feel her presence... I also found her birth record on micro-fiche. She *is* me! Her father's name was Robert, which is also on record. Mom had told me the name Robert (St.) James years ago. I saw Robert Philp's name on micro-fiche. He lived in Petworth! A person I completely made up out of the blue. He was born in 1664, two years before Katherine. What are the odds of finding names of people in a small town from three hundred years ago? I saw a John Baron that could have been John's grandfather. I also saw the name Hatchett from that time period and area. Where would I get the name Hatchett? It's a surname that I've never known anyone to have. And I didn't find this information out until *after* I'd written about these people; thinking I'd made up the whole thing. How in Hell could that happen? This is more than just a story."

"Coincidence?" Debbie asked.

"O.K., O.K.," I countered. "I wonder myself about the John Lennon part, but I believe in John Baron, I feel him. I trust he's here; now. Whether he is John Lennon, or connected to him or what, I don't really know, but the rest I'm pretty sure of. I have remembered a past life!"

"Looney-tunes, looney-tunes," Debbie mocked me in a sing-song voice.

I was stunned.

I stood up and in a cold, rasping voice, said, "Bitch." Neither expecting nor waiting for a reply, I strode out of the door.

It was only when I got home that I dissolved into tears. Maybe Debbie was right, maybe I'd gone completely off the deep end. But, if that were the case how could names of people that I had made up just happen to be on record from the 1600's in a tiny little village? The odds were too much. And what about feelings? I trust my feelings if someone makes me angry or sad. Shouldn't I also trust my feelings about the unseen, too?

After I had regained my composure, I dialed Debbie's number. Debbie, realizing it was me, assumed her superior manner. I was going to apologize, admit I was silly . . .

"No," I said, "I did not phone to apologize. I just called to tell you that we can no longer be friends. Good bye, Debbie." (I wonder now, years later, that I may have been too harsh but that was then . . . )

The next morning an envelope arrived postmarked 'Petworth'. Tearing it open, I read, "Your letter was forwarded to me from the Sussex Historical Society. I am the editor of a small journal we have in Petworth. This journal was established to preserve the character and history of Petworth. I suggest you join our society whereby you will be acquainted with Petworth's colorful history. For any further inquiries, please feel free to write me, or contact our secretary, Mrs. Ros Staker." It was signed, Mr. Peter Jerrome.

Mr. Jerrome had enclosed a copy of the "Petworth Journal" and as I stared at the painting of a village square on it's cover, I strangely felt at peace.

Over the next four years, Konni continued her conversations with John which she relayed to me through tapes and phone calls. And through these years, not only did I become more acquainted with John and Katherine's past, but I became re-acquainted with my sister.

Our tapes usually consisted of me sending her Beatle and Lennon songs which she would do a "reading" on. Usually, she picked up on various lifetimes John had had or she could feel the mood he had been in when the song had been written. I knew she had no Beatle music at her house, so I was always amazed at her accuracy of knowing whether or not John had written part or all of a song. Konni was unable to pick up anything from songs written by Paul. The idea to send these songs to her, first came to me when she had "seen" the same chimes as my Mother had, when listening to 'Jealous Guy'. I also verified with both of them and they agreed . . . they had never discussed this song with each other.

Our phone calls were because of slow mail; calls when she would have a message from John or I would have a question for him. The day calls weren't cheap and we both shared a dread of a husband's wrath over high phone bills! And when her bill became so high that the phone company cut her off completely, I conjured our father into sending her the exact amount of money needed for the bill as a birthday gift.

One day, I asked Konni what she thought of Mom's theory of feelings being the soul's memories of past lives.

"Sure," she said, "I feel more comfortable down here in the States. It just feels right for me . . . not a Canadian feeling to have, I know." She laughed, "So, I can relate to feelings."

"O.K.," I said, "But, there has to be more to this than feelings, right? I mean, you moved to where it felt right but most people wouldn't actually try to follow their feelings to the ends of the earth."

Konni laughed, "Yeah, but they try. Travel agencies make a fortune on people who simple *have* to get to a certain country. And for people who aren't trying to physically get somewhere, they try and create it with a certain style of clothes, a style of decor in their homes, or it's reflected in their interests and hobbies. Usually, odd traits are just an accumulation of a preferred type of life. The clues to one's past lives are endless."

I thought of Bob's brother, who scraped his money to travel to Jamaica time and time again. The Jamaica he travelled to wasn't the tourist resorts where exotic drinks and tanned North Americans were the norm. His Jamaica was as primitive as the dirt floored huts he stayed in and the fish and breadfruit his diet consisted of. I wondered if he was going back to a previous life ...a place he simply had to return to.

I wondered if some of my own traits and oddities were from past lives. I was the only woman I knew who didn't wear earrings. I hated to shop. I couldn't keep a garden alive but I did love wild flowers. I liked horses. I disliked sports. I loved waltzes. The color blue made me feel sad. If I could, I would live on fresh bread and cheese.

And my beginnings with Bob began in mystery. Weeks before I had actually met Bob, or spoken to him, he had seen me in a pub. I was told by a mutual acquaintance that he was interested, but this didn't alleviate the surprise of receiving a letter from him; a letter written in Old English (and red ink) about a stranger arriving at a Baron's Court and falling in love at a distance with a young lady there. Years later, Bob had no explanation as to why he'd written this letter in prose from centuries ago.

And what of Bob? His dark hair and beard accompanied by his tall, lanky frame made him look to be more of a sailor of days gone by, than a modern day train engineer. His interest in World War II was, in my opinion, a bit excessive but I wasn't one to talk about a compulsive interest in something!

For a time I began to see everybody in terms of what their past life connections may have been. I saw a neighbor who was not only interested in Tudor times but her physical appearance resembled someone from a Holbein's portrait ... and a friend whose home not only looked like a 1940s magazine but her general view of life reflected the same era.

I found this new concept fascinating but finally I decided to give up on everyone else's past lives for awhile and just concentrate on John's. I asked Konni to see all of John's lives that she could. Over the next few months she had various tidbits for me.

Konni related to me a time when John was a knight from

Wales. His name had been George. Another life, also in Wales, he and I had been twins with the surname Llewellyn. I checked out the name Llewellyn on micro-fiche and after finding hundreds of them, I quickly decided to stick with John and Katherine's life in Sussex. (I also did a quick check in an 'origin of names' book and discovered that in Wales the name Llewellyn was often shortened to Lewis!)

Konni saw several lives of John's spent as Jewish men in either New York or London. She told me of a life in London as a well-to-do man. One of his employees was a gardener, who in his present life is George Harrison.

I was intrigued with Konni's stories. Some days I was amazed, other days I thought, this all couldn't be true. I needed some different verification so as I had done so long ago, I asked Joanne a question. "Joanne," I said, "Aunt Konni has been telling me about some of John Lennon's past lives. I want to ask you some stuff about it too, O.K?"

Joanne, now a teenager, sighed, rolled her eyes, then obliged.

I started, "Konni sees that John had been a knight..."

She interrupted, "Not a knight in England...but a knight in Wales...and his name was George."

Alright, alright, I thought. Shortly after my verification from Joanne, I received a sign in the disguise of a Christmas gift. Bob's sister, who knew absolutely nothing of my search but only thought I was an old and odd Beatles' fan, unknowingly added to my list of strange happenings. I simply stared at the poster sized replica of the 'Revolver' album cover which consisted of a collage of the Beatles in photos, with inserted drawings. First, I noticed John in knight's armour. Then, a photo of John looking exactly like an elderly Jewish man. And lastly, was a photo of John but his pants had been drawn in...in plaid. I remembered Joanne saying, when she had first seen a spirit, "Mom...he's wearing plaid."

These strange happenings were interesting, but it was Katherine and John I wanted to get back to.

As the years went by, I began to feel frustrated that I was receiving my answers to questions through my sister. Not that I didn't appreciate the help. I will always be indebted to her, but I also had the need to look to myself for answers. I thought about it for a long time, not knowing how I could actually achieve this.

One day, I was so deep in thought I barely noticed a heavy rain against the window. The newspaper, blown from the step, was strewn like Kleenex all over the lawn. I threw on a raincoat and dashed out to rescue the paper. It was hopeless. Those pieces that I could gather up were so wet that I took the sodden mass to the garbage can. As I dropped it in, I noticed an advertisement for a "past life regression" by psychic, Laara Bracken. I thought of the psychic, Madeline, who had seen Patrick, and who had seen music when questioned about John. Of course . . . regression would be my next step. Without pausing to remove the dripping raincoat, I dashed to the telephone to make an appointment.

# Thirteen

I took a deep breath before I opened the motel door and met Laara. She looked a youthful fiftyish with soft blonde hair piled high on her head, her kind face reassured me about being regressed. Her smooth and confidant voice dismissed any remaining apprehensions I had about giving her an explanation of what had motivated me to try a regression.

Once I revealed to her that I knew the lifetime I hoped to experience... 1600's, in a village called Petworth, in Sussex, England, I was able, in ten minutes, to tell her the whole story. It was much easier telling it to this lady than to Bob or Debbie.

Laara fluffed up a pillow and motioned me to the nearby couch. She instructed me to relax and, as I lay back and felt the tension leave me, I heard her soft voice beside me. "Have a bell ring in your mind... and let that bell bring you to the significant lifetime which involved you with John Baron... and let that bell take you back to the village of Petworth, Sussex." Vaguely, I could hear Laara push 'play' on a tape recorder.

A car in the parking lot was revving it's motor and a light rain pattered against the window. Slowly the noises melted away as I approached a village in the center of green rolling hills. All was silent except for the barking of a dog.

After a long pause, she continued, "You are now in the village of Petworth, Sussex. What do you see?"

I could see buildings that were very close together but it wasn't very clear.

"Can you get closer?... What do you see?"

I saw a square... golden brown and dirty. There were cobblestones... but not modern cobblestones... just rocks put together.

"And the buildings?"

They were dirty, yet a gold color. They were not like the English towns we see now... all painted and pretty.

"What else do you see?"

I saw a dog... a little wild.

"Trees, grass or flowers?"

All I saw was a square with buildings... no greenery and a lane leading out of the square.

"Take a look down at yourself and tell me what you are wearing."

I was wearing a brownish golden dress... part should be white but it was dirty. My hair was long and dark.

"Are you wearing shoes?"

I couldn't tell... my dress hid my feet.

"How old are you?"

Fifteen.

"Do you have a name?"

Katherine.

"You are fifteen years old and your name is Katherine? What are you doing in the square?"

I did not know. I did not live there. I seemed to be holding something like a basket. Then I could see more clearly. I seemed to be waiting for someone to come out of one of the houses. I was afraid of the dog because it seemed wild.

"Is there anything in your basket?"

I had bread or buns... little loaves of bread. That was what the dog wanted.

"Where did you get the bread?"

I did not know.

"Look out of Katherine's eyes... down at the basket... where did the basket of bread come from?"

I replied that it was from my aunt... not my house.

Laara was now addressing me as "Katherine" and I was responding naturally and easily as she continued the questioning. "Katherine, do you know someone named John Baron?"

I did not.

"All right, you are fifteen . . . Go ahead five years to when you are twenty."

I was dead.

" . . . Katherine, what do you see? Look down at yourself and tell me what you are wearing."

I was buried. I was wearing a light brown dress.

Laara was momentarily startled when she realized that I had gone beyond Katherine's life. "Go back to when you are fifteen and you are in Petworth, Sussex, and you have a basket of bread. Do you know what year it is, Katherine?"

1681.

"I'd like you to go ahead, one year to 1682, when you are sixteen. Tell me where you are."

In the garden.

"What are you doing in the garden?"

I was wandering through the tall flowers.

"Do you know someone named John Baron?"

Yes, I did.

"We'll move ahead a month. Now, Katherine, tell me where you are."

On a picnic.

"Who's with you?"

John. He is standing by a horse . . . it's hitched to a plain carriage by a tree . . . he is untying the horse.

"Are there other people around?"

No.

"He takes care of the horse and then, what happens?"

We act like children, running in the grass. I giggled with the recollection. Then, as quickly, a deep sob wracked my body as I realized that we had not been happy since that afternoon.

"How do you know that?"

I don't know *how* I knew that . . . I just did.

"You are running about in the grass, acting like children. What else do you ?"

We talked, laughed and ate. We made love. I could feel the sun on our bodies, smell the earthy odor of the grass, I could smell John! A mixture of fresh air and leather. I could feel John! Rough skin, soft hair.

We had to go back; I had to go home. My parents did not know where I was.

"Stop. Before you go home ... I want you to go over to him ... you can do this now ... go over to him ... take his hands and look into his eyes ... what do you see?"

I saw John's blue eyes; sandy hair; chiselled features; high cheek bones.

"Do you love him?"

Yes.

"He loves you?"

Yes.

"How do you know?"

I know.

"Are you going to be married?"

There were lots of barriers; including parents.

"Why are they against your marrying?"

I did not know; but it was something about John's health. I didn't want to talk about it; I didn't want to face the memory.

" ... does John take you home or do you return on your own?"

We went together; he saw me home. He was not afraid of my parents as I was ... nobody saw us ... except perhaps a servant, but she won't say anything.

"Then what happens?"

He got ill.

"What happens?"

He died.

"How long after your picnic?"

It was a few months later. John died from consumption ... what we now call tuberculosis.

"Do you blame anyone?"

The country ... for being so wet and cold.

"How do you react to his death?"

I couldn't think straight. Someone seems to be holding me a prisoner; a woman who does not want me to know the truth. Oh, God . . . I was wrong . . . I did not look after John in the hospital. After he got ill, my parents used his illness as a convenient way to pressure his grandfather to have him sent away and I never saw him again. After he was gone, my parents told me he had died.

My parents had promised me that my Auntie would take care of me. She would make the hurt go away . . . but she kept me so drugged, my very memories are wrong . . . I confused my working in the hospital with tending to John . . . I *did* work in a hospital and John *did* die but I've put the two incidents together . . .

Now, I'm a prisoner in my own room. I started gasping, Auntie, Auntie, no more medicine! I tried to visualize Auntie, and then, Debbie! I saw Debbie in the room with my Aunt Agatha.

I could no longer answer Laara's questions.

Debbie was called Rachel. Rachel had been hiding, and when my Auntie left she gave me more medicine. I tried to tell her that I had already had my medicine, but I could not speak. I could not think. Everything was fuzzy. I was dying . . . I could see John waiting for me. I had a split second understanding: Rachel (or was it Debbie?) was jealous of me . . . she, too, loved John . . . and for that she would see me dead.

"Jewelle . . . Jewelle, I want you to leave the situation and go back to the time when you and John are at the picnic. I would like you to picture a white light wrapping itself around both of you and taking you away. You do not have to go through that pain again. The same white light is now being sent to the picnic area and is healing all from that moment to this moment. Let all the old grief turn to loving energy and know that the rift between you and your soul mate has now been healed . . . See yourself as whole . . . both male and female . . . John and Jewelle."

I was back in the room with Laara, lying on the beige couch with the pillow under my head. I heard the tape recorder click to a stop. I was surprised to find my cheeks were damp. Although I was dizzy as I sat up, I was thinking very clearly. I had to go home . . . to Petworth . . . I had to go home.

# Fourteen

My view of Katherine's life had changed. When writing Katherine's story I had a bittersweet romantic remembrance of her time with John. However, the regression took my memories and made me feel fully her life in the 1600's. Through Katherine's eyes I was aware of having no concept of the world, outside of Petworth. I was surprised at how my perception of life three hundred years ago had changed by experiencing it. Petworth in the 1600's was drab and dirty, people worked hard and played hard, lives were short and futures uncertain. I was aware that Katherine accepted her primitive conditions in the same way we accept the many flaws of living in the twentieth century.

I had reached a crossroads. To complete my search once and for all, I would have to go back to England. I couldn't continue chasing shadows. I needed to know whether I had lived in this Sussex town, whether I had known John and a hundred other details.

This was my final decision. If I came to a dead end as I had in Mere, I would put the whole thing away knowing I'd experienced the ultimate delusion. If I succeeded, I would write a book for those like-minded people I knew were out there. If I could reach one person who may be experiencing what I have, my purpose would have been accomplished.

I dropped hints to Bob that maybe another trip overseas was in order, saying I needed to check out Katherine and John's past life once more. Bob hinted in return that if I earned the money, that may be a good place to start!

September, 1989, I started a part-time job at an elementary school where my youngest daughter, Kristy, attended. Every day as I walked to school, I knew I walked one step closer to finding my answers. Other days, when I wondered if there were any answers, my mood would be uplifted by viewing the world through the innocent eyes of young children.

I began to prepare for the last mile of my search. I had learned from my experience at Mere; my only focus in England would have to be Petworth, that I would have to stay there, not just drop in casually for an afternoon.

My first and only contact, Peter Jerrome, who, months earlier had sent me copies of the historic "Petworth Journal", was the first to be contacted. I wrote to him under the guise of doing family research on the James' family in the 1600's.

Through my genealogy group, I found the address for the Sussex Record Office. Not only did I enquire of Katherine James, but of small aspects of Katherine's story. I felt ridiculous trying to find the right words. How could I ask whether laudanum was abused by indifferent aunts? Or how many people have you on record that fell in love at the balls held in the Great Hall? Or was there even a Great Hall or ... or? Finally I compiled questions that I hoped were general, trying to sound professional.

Throughout this time of seeking information I continued my many phone calls to California. My sister insisted that John would like me to try communicating with him myself. How was I supposed to do that? Konni said, "Be calm, lie down in a quiet room, close your eyes and he will be with you." I tried. I would get a vague impression of him but was it my imagination? Sometimes I would drift off to sleep, dreaming that we were dancing, but aren't dreams just another way of imagining, or are they? Suddenly, one day I saw him vividly and I didn't hesitate to wonder if this was real. I visualized myself leaving my body.

83

My spirit joined with his as we looked down on planet Earth. He took my hand and said, "Would you like to see Petworth? I'll take you there."

As we approached the English town, I could see a soft pinkish glow in the distance. As we came closer my attention focused on a church spire, glowing in the same pink hue, that rose proudly and protectively above Petworth. Then, instantly, all was gone and I was back on my bed. Had I been seeing things? Why was everything all pink? I decided my imagination was getting better and better all the time!

Months later, I read this tidbit in an English book, on various villages in Sussex. I realized I could only accept that there is so much more to this world than I'll ever begin to understand.

"The church in Petworth, on the highest point in town, is an architectural mixture of many ages. There is no trace of the Saxon church the Norman registers noted, but there are echoes of the thirteenth and fourteenth centuries. What makes the greatest impact on your vision is the strong tower.

The stone base is medieval. Sir Charles Barry added the top part of *pinkish-red* brick in the early nineteenth century, and he also replaced the faltering spire with a new one which became a landmark, easily picked out above the surrounding hills, valleys, woodlands and meadows. But this, too, weakened, became a danger and was taken down in 1947."

Pinkish-red brick? The spire taken down in 1947? What did this mean? I'd heard of the concept of no time and I suspected this was some proof of that concept. Again, I simply had to accept that my visualizing this pink tower couldn't have been imagination.

Peter Jerrome's letter arrived. His reply was that the James' family was a large and scattered one through this part of Sussex in the 1600s. He had enclosed a book titled, "Cloakbag and Common Purse," about a "William James who in the late 1500s in Petworth, was a tenant's leader in a court battle with Henry Percy, 9th Earl of Northumberland, who had allegedly enclosed illegally his tenant's copyhold land in Petworth."

It was interesting that a member of the James family was

referred to as a "tantalizing figure in Petworth's history" and I wondered exactly what relation that he may have been to Katherine. I was also interested to note the author of the book was Peter Jerrome himself!

The next few months brought bits and pieces of information from the Records Office. They were . . . "In the 1600s there was a Great Hall, in which many entertainments would take place . . . this Hall no longer exists, Petworth House having been re-built. The only hospital in Petworth in the 1600s was Thompson's Hospital, founded in 1624 for the maintenance of twelve poor persons. There would be a Matron. There are no lists of inmates before the 19th Century. Laudanum was invented by Paracelsus (d. 1541)."

I not only learned that the spelling of personal names weren't yet standardized but the name of Petworth had been varied itself through the centuries, with the first name coming from a Saxon derivative, "Pytta's enclosure". Domesday Book mentions Peterode. In 1205, Peiteworth. Putworth in Edward I's time, Petteworth in medieval days and in Henry the VIII's time, Pettewoorth.

I learned, too, that a manor had always been the center point of Petworth, with the great house first being mentioned in the year 791. A thousand years later, Petworth House was still the focal point in Petworth. (This boggled my mind as I looked around at my own surroundings in B.C. that had barely existed a hundred years ago.)

I was absolutely fascinated with the history of this town. I felt I couldn't wait any longer to try and find answers. Although I had been working and saving money, I didn't have nearly enough saved to travel to England, but I simply had to go.

I approached Bob, expecting an argument. He surprised me by looking at me intently and saying, "You really have to go, don't you?" Before I could reply, he said, "Go . . . do it, get it over with."

Before he could change his mind, I phoned the travel agency and booked a flight in September. My Visa bill was my second guilt. My first was leaving Bob alone once more, as I set off to again try and solve my past life losses.

Remembering Peter Jerrome's advice of long ago, 'for more information, write to our secretary of the Petworth Journal, Mrs. Staker.' I did just that, asking her to please send me tourist information. A few weeks later, Mrs. Staker not only sent me a town guide but also an invitation to drop in for coffee whenever I arrived.

I thumbed through the small guide at the listings of bed and breakfasts, when one caught my eye. 'Minutes from town, a Tudor town house...' I immediately wrote, asking for a reservation in the last week in September.

I was days away from my departure; I was excited and nervous, everything was at stake. This would be the trip that would tell my fate, whether I would give up the whole search or carry it to the end.

My bags were packed and everything was in order. Minutes before leaving the house, Konni phoned. "Hi, I'm glad I caught you before you left. John just told me to remind you of the bluebells. He says you loved them. They grow wild... fields of them in the woods... maybe you'll see them."

"Bluebells," I laughed. "O.K., I'll add them to my list."

I arrived at Gatwick Airport on a warm and sunny afternoon in September, 1990. I would follow the route I had planned for months; take a train from the airport to Pulborough, the nearest train station to Petworth; take a cab the last five miles to Petworth. The whole route wouldn't take more than an hour.

Tears came to my eyes as we sped south through the rolling green Sussex countryside sprinkled with majestic oak trees and grazing sheep. The scenery was exactly as I had remembered when writing Katherine's story. I knew I was nearly home.

I wiped my eyes, and gathered my bags, as we pulled into Pulborough station. The train door wouldn't open! There was no conductor in sight as I tugged and pushed at the door. "God damn it," I muttered, panic setting in. Once again the fast train was moving, pulling out of the station. Feeling like a fool, I approached the only other passenger, a woman about my age. My voice was quivering. I was shaking, "I couldn't get the door open... where is the next station?"

"Amberly. The doors are child proof . . . you have to put your hand through the window and open it from the outside."

A variety of unkind thoughts directed at Britrail sped through my head as I thanked the woman who helped with the door at the next stop.

The fast train stopped only long enough for me to quickly alight onto a platform, then swished out of sight. I looked around at my surroundings but there was not a person in sight at the seemingly abandoned railway station. The dark red building decorated with an abundance of flower boxes sat shimmering in the sunshine. I looked through the station windows and tried the doors. Everything was locked. A sign on the door said it opened at 5:00. 'Great,' I thought, it was only 2:00. Dejectedly I limped along, with heavy luggage in tow, across an overhead footpath that took me to the platform on the opposite side of the tracks. I would just have to wait for a train going back to Pulborough.

I sat on a bench, my only company a bee that droned around a nearby flower box. Total exhaustion and the whole ludicrous situation was too much for me and I began sobbing.

Drained, I wiped away my tears and then stared in disbelief. I hadn't noticed that directly in front of me, back across the train track, were massive white chalk cliffs. I stood in awe. White cliffs several feet away! I remembered the very first time my Mom had told me about John and Katherine – I recalled her words, "I see white cliffs, fog and lush green grass." For a long time I sat alone in the presence of the stark white cliffs and I knew that I'd missed my train station for the purpose of simply arriving at these cliffs.

Hoisting my bags to the most comfortable position possible, I left, walking down a short lane. I came to a beautiful stone house with a massive garden overflowing with color. An elderly lady answered the door and again I had to control my tears. "Hi, I just arrived from Canada . . . I got off at the wrong station and I'm trying to get to Petworth. Could you please call me a cab?"

Hesitantly, the woman asked me to wait a minute as she called to her husband. I pretended not to notice their obvious suspicion as I repeated my problem. After a few moments, he offered, "I will drive you to Petworth."

I sat back and relaxed as we turned off the highway, to a smaller road which had a sign indicating Petworth, 5 miles. Minutes later, the elderly gentleman came to a stop in front of Grange House. I thanked him for his kindness and with a cheery "Good Luck" he left me on the sidewalk.

# *Fifteen*

The white Georgian faced house, which was to be my bed and breakfast lodgings, was smaller than I had expected. Responding to my rap on the heavy door, a pretty young woman greeted me warmly and invited me into the sitting room.

A grand rustic fireplace dominated the tiny room, dwarfing the stuffed sofa and chairs. What caught my attention was the pram sitting in the middle of the room.

"My daughter...she's seven weeks old," said the proud mother. "Would you like a cup of coffee or tea?"

As I sat in the cozy kitchen, drinking tea and chatting with my hostess, I felt comfortable and so glad I had finally arrived in Petworth.

To her query about visiting my family, I explained, "No, I do not have family here but I'm doing family research. I'm into genealogy and tracing my family tree."

At her polite but disinterested response, I knew we had exhausted conversation. I gulped down my tea and suggested that I would like to settle into my room. Grabbing one of my bags, my hostess led the way up the stairs. I was aware of a faint aroma, a blend of potpourri and furniture polish. The staircase which led from the sitting room was steep and narrow, typical of ancient houses. The landlady announced that she would put me in the top attic room so that the baby wouldn't disturb me.

Oddly, a sense of foreboding suddenly came over me when we started the ascent of the second flight of stairs. Nearing the top, the stairs took a sharp turn. I felt an icy chill run through my body. I experienced a reluctance to go any further but, nevertheless, I followed the landlady into the room that was to be home for the following week. I was bid to watch my head as we entered the attic room. My hostess departed after inviting me to have a bath if I wished. I sat down on the huge wooden framed bed and looked around the room. It had thick beams supporting the slanted ceiling. I wondered if the wrought iron chandelier was salvaged from a dungeon somewhere. The long narrow window above my head provided a beautiful view of Petworth House and the surrounding town in the distance. I felt silly about my momentary sense of panic and was glad my hostess did not detect it. Guessing that fatigue was to blame, I chose to have the suggested hot bath. After a long soak, I donned jeans and a sweater, announced that I was off to walk around Petworth and set out to see all I could.

Narrow ancient lanes wound this way and that; traces of medieval times were everywhere. Quaint stone cottages had tiny garden plots filled with colorful flowers. There were lace curtains adorning most windows, and milk bottles waiting on doorsteps. The lanes, like erratic spokes to a wheel, converged on a large square where the many shops vied for every available bit of frontage. Dodging the traffic which pinwheeled about me, I cut across the square and entered a particularly narrow alley which twisted into a much smaller square, only paces from the first.

I stood rooted to the spot; this was the square I saw in my regression. It was here I was Katherine, holding a basket of bread, the buildings around, my dress, the cobblestones . . . all the same golden brown color. I had wondered why the scene had been all one hue. Now, as I looked about me, I had no doubt this was the same square. A brass sign, hanging from a corner post, read, "Golden Square." Had I been seeing things in a kind of symbolic color in the regression the same way I had seen Petworth in a pink hue when looking at the old church tower? An interesting concept. One I didn't understand but nevertheless a concept that had definitely happened to me twice.

On the opposite side of the square was an arrow pointing to Petworth House. Once more, dodging traffic, I found myself at the huge wooden door at the front entrance. I followed a small crowd of people inside.

Barely aware of the Van Dycks and Turners and the other decor, I suddenly felt disoriented and sought refuge of a nearby bench and railed, 'What in Hell am I doing here? What kind of idiot am I . . . coming all this way, hoping to find some stupid clue? I was through all of this before at Mere.'

I sat on the bench for what seemed like a long time, staring into space. Finally, I bade myself move and found myself in a long, narrow corridor with a low ceiling. The walls were covered with many black plaques. I was aware of feeling a strange mixture of calm and apprehension. I was most certainly reacting intuitively to these surroundings. I hastened through the corridor and out into the late afternoon sun. I stood for awhile staring back at the magnificent building; feeling nothing familiar about the stone exterior. I was almost relieved.

I strolled through the manicured lawns and rounding the corner of Petworth House, I saw St. Mary's church a stone's throw away. Here was the same church I'd seen on my "trip" with John, not at a distance this time, but right in front of me. I quickly entered the quiet churchyard. With growing excitement, I approached the enormous wooden door and pushed it open.

The only light came filtered through stained glass windows, casting odd shadows on tattered and worn pew cushions. On one wall were plaques commemorating people from days gone by. No matter how hard I tried, I could not seem to feel any link with this cold dark place. As I was about to leave, I was startled by a tall, thin woman who slid past me carrying a pile of papers. I called her, explaining that I was doing research on various old Petworth families. I asked to see the church records from the l660's and wished to see the Vicar if he was in.

"Well, I'm sorry," she replied in a clipped manner, "the Vicar is not in today. And, anyway, there are no records kept here . . . the original records are much too valuable to just let anybody look at, aren't they? You will have to go to the Records Office in Chichester to look at anything from this Parish."

I wandered slowly around the churchyard, observing ancient and decaying tombstones. Modern Petworth was hidden from view by lush green oak trees and as I looked at the headstones, I wondered if any of the James family was buried here . . . or John . . . or me? Was I looking at my own grave and not knowing it? (Four years later, my last verification was a letter received from the Record Office that stated Katherine James, daughter of Robert James, was buried in St. Mary's Churchyard. 1683! Most tombstones were illegible but indeed I had been looking at my very own burial site, without knowing it.)

I sat in that church garden, mulling things over until the sun began to set and a chill came to the air. (Throughout my stay, I often would wander through the cemetery that surrounded the church and for brief seconds at a time, I could nearly touch ghosts from the past.)

I followed ancient Lombard Street, a cobblestone lane, back to Market Square to a Tudor tea shop and ordered tea and fruitcake. I consulted my notebook which contained my list of places I wanted to see. But at that moment, it was human contact I needed. I thought of Mrs. Staker, who had sent tourist information about Petworth and had enclosed a note saying, "When you are in Petworth, drop in for coffee." Not used to dropping in on people unannounced, I decided to go before I lost my nerve. I paid for the tea and asked directions to #29 Green Lane.

The semi-detached house looked cozy and inviting but I found myself wondering, as I knocked on the door, whether Mrs. Staker would be strange, or worse, rich and eccentric!

Answering the door was a robust woman dressed in a traditional English grey tweed skirt accented by a cream colored blouse. I hesitantly introduced myself, saying I had just arrived from Canada and reminded her of the pamphlets she had sent. Her conservative dress, however, was not reflected in her manner.

Her twinkling blue eyes and wide smile warmly greeted me as she invited me in, offering to make coffee.

Mrs. Staker looked at me thoughtfully. "This is the strangest thing. Just this morning, I thought 'Mrs. Lewis . . . I wonder when she will arrive?' Funny . . . and here you are."

She had me sit at an oval table covered with a crisp linen cloth and disappeared into the kitchen for coffee. I immediately felt at home. From the kitchen, my hostess remarked, "I just can't get over thinking about you only this morning. I had pictured you as being about 70, very rich . . . the kind of woman who travels a lot, dabbling in different curiosities. So what exactly are you doing in Petworth?"

Asking her to please call me 'Jewelle', I launched into my story. "I am here because I am sure that I lived another life in Petworth, three hundred years ago. I am trying to check that out. Coming to Petworth is the last stage of my search." Within minutes, I had poured out the whole story to this warm English lady who already seemed like a friend. However, I omitted my suspicions about being connected to John Lennon.

Mrs. Staker responded by saying it was quite a story and she knew just the people I should meet, starting with Peter Jerrome of the Petworth Society. "Yes," I told her, "his was one of the names on my list." She added Jumbo Taylor, a nice chap, who probably knew more about Petworth history than anybody.

I couldn't believe the interest this woman was taking in me, as she talked about different people who could help. I had the strange feeling that all of this had been staged and all I had to do was go along with the script.

I asked her if she had time to do all this for me.

"Gads, yes," she explained, "this kind of thing doesn't happen every day. So what did you do today, then?"

I told her about my rather weird first day; how I had familiar feelings about Golden Square, the corridor at Petworth House and the Churchyard. "I would start to choke up at nearly every corner. I am sure that half the population has noticed this foreign woman blubbering her way across town . . . Mrs. Staker, I am so glad I have met you!"

"Mrs. Staker! . . . Blimey, please call me Ros."

She offered to walk me back to my lodgings since the street was very dark. The winding lane was a little eery, being lit only by a pale moon, so the company was appreciated. It was a pleasant evening and with the day's roar of traffic through the village silenced, the only sound was our chatter.

As we neared my bed and breakfast, I told Ros that I had been using two ways of putting my story together . . . first getting information from psychics and then trying to check it out factually with proof. I was in Petworth in order to get some black and white proof.

"Well, maybe not," Ros said, "I know of a psychic who is very good. She lives in Tillington, a mile or so away from here."

At my eager reaction, she promised to see what she could do about arranging a meeting. At that, we bade each other good night and I entered my bed and breakfast.

The warmth and aroma of the roaring fire in the fireplace followed me up the first flight of stairs to my attic room.

However, on the second flight, I felt a cold chill; the feeling slowly subsided after settling into my room.

I was out of my clothes quickly. Taking a new white flannel nightgown from my bag, I slowly let it fall over my head. I imagined myself having thick, dark hair cascading down my back. I recall thinking that exhaustion does funny things to one's mind, as I fell into the bed, instantly asleep.

# *Sixteen*

I woke to a still and quiet room. Stretching lazily, I groped for my watch. It was nearly noon! As I took a quick bath, I mentally planned my day. After applying make-up and dressing for action, I flew down both flights of stairs.

In the kitchen, my hostess greeted me with, "Oh, good morning ... or, should I say 'good afternoon'?"

Still feeling the effects of jet lag, I declined breakfast, asking only for juice. Serving me a glass of cold orange juice, she said, "A lady named Ros Staker was here this morning. She left a message for you to meet her at her work place at 12:30. She left a map. It's a brick building between Market Square and Golden Square and has a sign: 'Dr. Morrow – Dentist.'

12:30! That was minutes away! I gulped down the juice, thanked my landlady, and dashed out the door.

I was aware of blue skies and warm air as I walked swiftly along the lanes toward the large square. I found the red brick building and as I entered, I encountered Ros, wearing a white medical coat and a broad smile.

"Your landlady said you were crashed out; Jewelle, I would like you to meet Ann ... we work together. We have finished up here for the day, so I thought we could all have lunch together. There's a pub just around the corner."

Ann was an attractive blonde woman in her forties. As she

95

shed her medical coat, I noticed that, unlike Ros' more conservative dress of tweed and wool, Ann could pass for an American, donned in jeans and a bright sweatshirt.

I could tell that these women were more than fellow workers; they shared a sparkle and wit, which they included me in. I felt as comfortable with Ann as I had meeting Ros.

To my relief, because I was getting tired of repeating myself, Ros had already told Ann my story.

The pub was dark and quiet; small oval tables faced an unlit fireplace. The few patrons spoke no louder than in whispers.

"It's like a ruddy morgue in here, isn't it?" commented Ros. Seeing no sign of a waitress, she strode up to the bar to see about lunch herself. Ann and I found a table and sat down.

"So, Jewelle, you have come all this way to check this out? Fascinating. My daughter would be interested in your story. She has a "gift" as we call it. When she was young she would often be frightened by spirits who would approach her, but now she can talk to spirits as easily as I am talking to you. She is quite private about it and only talks about her experiences within our family. I am sure she would be interested in you."

I couldn't believe it! Ros, last night, telling me of a psychic who lived close by and now Ann telling me of her daughter, Becky, who has a psychic "gift."

Ros triumphantly returned, armed with pub lunches and gin and tonics for all. As she sat down, she informed me that she had made arrangements for us to meet the psychic that evening. "I told Pet briefly why you are here and . . ."

"Her name is Pet? . . . as in Petworth?"

"Well, no, actually it's Petula, and she's looking forward to meeting you."

Petula lived in a neighboring village, Tillington, but thought it better to see me in Petworth since that was where I felt I had lived. We were to meet at the dentist's office where Ann and Ros worked. Because that building dated from the 1600's, Pet felt it might have vibrations from that time. I wondered if Ann was to be there; she admitted that she would be interested, if I didn't mind. I felt it natural that both she and Ros be there and said so.

As we sat and chatted, I felt a deep sense of belonging. Taking a deep breath, I stated that I should tell them something more before we saw the psychic that evening. When I indicated that the fellow I was involved with in the 1660's might be the same soul as John Lennon, Ros and Ann glanced quickly at each other. Suddenly scared, I wondered whether they thought I might be a nut case.

"You know," Ann said, "I'm sure that Paul McCartney has a home in Sussex."

Was she making fun of me? I added, emphatically, that Paul McCartney had absolutely nothing to do with my story.

Suddenly, we all laughed at the thought; dissolving any remaining tension I had felt.

I went on to tell the two women of how, for four years after John Lennon was killed, I had been in a state of perpetual grief. Grieving for someone I had never met! If I had been a fan, it might have made some sense. But even fans don't think of someone every single day.

Finally, I explained, when I couldn't stand it any longer, I had asked a psychic if there was any reason for this grief. To make a long story short, I got the names and dates of ancient people connected with me and here I was in Petworth. I still had one very big question that I hadn't voiced aloud: Are/were John Baron and John Lennon one and the same soul ... or did John Lennon's death merely trigger some memory?

"Well," said Ros, draining the last of her gin, "Maybe Pet can answer some of your questions tonight. I'm glad I didn't know of the John Lennon part when I talked to her. This way, she can pick up whatever there is, without any preconceived ideas. In an hour though I've also arranged a visit with Peter Jerrome, our editor of the Petworth Society Journal."

Ann and Ros chatted on about local gossip and I felt like I had always sat here in the Angel pub, chatting away with old friends.

As we left the dark pub, back in the bright sunshine, Ann suggested that we go to the cemetery at the end of the lane and look for ancient names. From the lane, we entered a small alley leading to an unkept cemetery. We found ourselves knee high in brittle grass which caught at our feet and made the headstones barely visible. It was evident from the inscriptions that we were able to uncover, that this burial ground dated only from the 1800s.

We continued walking along the alley. Without warning, the village abruptly ended. In awe, I saw that we stood on a slight ridge overlooking a valley of soft green grass shimmering in the afternon sun. Later I learned that this shimmering valley is called the Shimmings Valley. Never had I seen a more beautiful sight. As we silently single filed our way down the path, I became aware that there was something familiar in the distance and asked the others if it was a road.

We focused our attention on what was but a faint trace of a road which branched off the path on which we stood and wound it's way across the valley and disappeared on the opposite side. Ros ventured that it was likely the ancient, long abandoned road to Fittleworth. Before us, our path looped through a wooded area and back into the village. I felt compelled to glance over my shoulder at the ancient route. As Ros and Ann chatted on, I drifted along in their wake, lost in thought.

Noticing my silence, Ros inquired whether I was nervous about meeting Pet. "No," I said slowly. "I'm just so confused about my familiar feelings I had when seeing the corridor to Petworth House and St. Mary's churchyard. The sight of the valley and its ancient road also gave me these mixed emotions."

Wistfully, Ros commented that the valley probably looked the same now as it did three hundred years ago.

Then suddenly, aware of the time, she said good bye to Ann and steered me in the direction of Peter Jerrome's. Ann went around the corner and disappeared into one of the many lanes off Market Square while Ros and I approached the doorway of a small shop.

A tinkling bell announced our entry; a petite woman behind a counter looked up and responded to Ros' greetings and introduction. Marian indicated that she anticipated our visit but was a bit puzzled, as was Peter, about why we wanted to talk to him. She locked the shop door. "I do say, though, I am quite intrigued. Please, do come in."

She led us up a short flight of stairs, through a maze of unusually shaped rooms, into a small, chilly sitting room. She invited us to sit down and went to inform Mr. Jerrome that we had arrived. I chose a stuffed chair opposite a ground level window which looked out on a garden bursting with color. In the quiet, as Ros and I waited, I heard the ticking of an unseen clock.

Peter Jerrome entered; a tall, spare man in his fifties, inclining his head to one side, betraying an inquisitive nature. Although he had the reserved, polite manner, characteristic of English men, I sensed a doubtfulness in his expression as Ros introduced us.

"Ros tells me that you believe you lived in Petworth... in another life, you say?"

At Ros' urging I started into my story, "Well, about ten years ago, a well known person was killed..." Whereupon, Ros interjected that it didn't matter *who* it was... just a well known individual died. "...after years of this unexplainable grief, I undertook trying to find the reasons for myself."

I told my whole story, detail by detail, trying to stick with the highlights of my search. Marian had served steaming tea in dainty china and was sitting, listening, wide-eyed as I concluded, "...so I have come to Petworth to see what I can learn of these people and places... Katherine James... and others."

Peter acknowledged the difficulty of the 1600's being such a remote time and asked for the names. I listed: Katherine James, her father Robert James, a Mr. Hatchett, Robert Philp and a John Baron from Fittleworth.

Peter zeroed in on Robert Philp.

"Robert Philp, you say? Born when?"

"1664."

"Well," Peter smiled for the first time, "this is his house in which we are sitting."

Ros' exclamation of surprise equalled my own as I realized that I was looking at my first tangible connection with Katherine.

Then, in a split second, I saw my 17th century friend. Robert Philp was Peter Jerrome!

"What does your husband think of all this, Mrs. Lewis?"

Such a typical male question! Keeping a straight face, I told Peter of Bob's skepticism, natural to someone of his pragmatic nature, which had started to weaken somewhat as 'proof' of the existence of these people started falling into place.

That elicited little response from Peter. He rose from the chair, said that it was very nice meeting me and that he really had to get back to his afternoon work. I was not surprised at the abrupt end to our meeting and watched with a feeling of fondness as this old friend departed the room, waving off our thank-yous. Marian saw us to the door; Peter had disappeared into his maze of rooms. As she unlocked the door, she said, "I am afraid Peter is a little skeptical about these things, but I found your story to be just delightful." The little bell tinkled at our departure.

We were standing at the edge of the square, each analyzing what we had just experienced. Ros voiced her impression that it was hard to tell what Peter was thinking.

She suggested going to her place for tea before we visited Pet. I assured her that, although I had put a lot of hope on his being the one who would answer all my questions, Peter had given me an unexpected piece of information regarding Robert Philp's house. I did not say that not only had I seen Robert Philp's house, I had also seen Robert Philp!

# Seventeen

We sat in Ros' cozy dining room, drinking hot tea and nibbling biscuits. I asked, "Tell me about Pet. I am picturing an older woman with a shawl and heavy jewellery."

Ros threw her head back as she laughingly refuted that image. "Pet is just an ordinary person; thirty, married with kids, talkative, observant. I sometimes forget that she is doing a reading. Then unexpectedly, she will say something such as seeing a spirit beside me or something connected to me."

I admitted a growing apprehension about seeing Pet, and how I felt that way every time I had consulted a psychic. I was always worried about what I would be told. Yet, I still was willing to take that chance.

Unlike this morning, I studied the ancient red brick building as we approached the dentist's office. I was fascinated by the idea that Katherine would have passed this very building many times in her lifetime.

Ann and Pet were waiting for us in the receptionist's room. I suddenly felt shy as Ros introduced me to the tall graceful woman with a long strawberry pony tail, who barely looked twenty. "Thanks for seeing me," I said.

Completely putting me at ease, she laughed and said warmly, "Really, it's my pleasure."

We all sat in big overstuffed chairs in the dentist's waiting room and quickly the mood changed. Pet took a deep breath and looked intently at me. "I am getting strong vibrations related to you. Yes, I see you a very long time ago in Petworth, as a young girl ... you are petite, have long dark hair. Your father, a merchant, though not of their class, is nevertheless accepted by the gentry. There is an elderly aunt ... either in your home or nearby ... you have met a young man with whom you are falling in love. He is from an aristocratic family but socializes with your family. He is physically frail; he is often ill; his future is unclear. Not only physically frail; he's thought of as being slightly mad. He is not mad ... he's just different but gets labelled, anyway. You, however, find him fascinating, listening to his thoughts about life and you spend many hours with him, just walking and talking.

"At first your parents think your friendship quite harmless ... but soon they become quite concerned when they hear whisperings of marriage. Not only is he sickly, but he is only the third son. If he dies and you have married, you will be left with nothing. Your parents begin to pressure his family to keep him away from you, by whatever means necessary.

"Despite your fear of your parents, you begin to meet this young man in secrecy. This is not easy when you both have servants, spinster aunts and nosy friends who are more than willing to report on you. However, you do have an older brother who adores you and helps you get away from your home, enabling you to meet with your love. Your brother's name is either Robert or John."

(Later on micro-fiche I found a John James, christened May 21, 1665 in Petworth ... Father, Robert ... he had been nine months older than Katherine.)

"It is impossible to meet in the village, so you now begin meeting on the outskirts and, alone, you travel by cart into the country. He often has packages of food prepared by his cook. Your picnics together become very special. Opposition from your parents grows greater ... I see the young man's grandfather here ... forced to send his grandson away. Since the young man is already thought of as ill, an excuse is readily made. He is allowed to see you once more to say good bye and to explain to you the necessity of his going to a rest home. His health has not been good, so this is perfectly understandable. What he does not know, is that arrangements have been made for his placement in an asylum.

"A few weeks go by; you are called to the sitting room in your family's home ... I see an enormous, elegant room with a white stone fireplace, heavy blue drapes and white and blue panels on the walls. On one wall are long windows that overlook a terraced garden. Here you are given the news of his death. You cry, you scream, and are wild with fury. Your behavior is totally inexcusable and after a few days, no longer tolerated. In your parent's view, you are being a silly nuisance. You are sent to live with an aunt. I see this aunt quite clearly ... she is a tall, thin, cold woman, dressed in black, a white cap on her head. You call her Aunt Agatha. She is unmoved by your grief and has only one solution ... to give you laudanum, an opium solution, given for all pain ... whether it be physical or mental. You are soon addicted and although your aunt is ignorant of the signs ... sweating and coughing ... she still looks after you. She thinks she has succeeded where your parents have failed. You are no longer raving, but are quite tranquil. Your small body, not able to endure a prolonged drugged state, becomes increasingly frail. You die peacefully one afternoon, many weeks after hearing of the death of your young man ... I should tell you that if he had not died, you would have both done whatever was necessary to be together. You would have run away to another part of England."

I sat, quite stunned, as if emerging from a dream. The detailed scene Pet had described seemed so vivid and real, yet all I could manage to say was, "The room where I was told of his death was blue ... the color blue has always made me so very sad ..."

Pet leaned toward me and quietly asked me if she could guess who the young man from the 1600's was. She could see him clearly ... before he was killed in this last life and that right now he was part of the room, part of Petworth, he was completely surrounding us. "He is John Lennon."

There was total silence in the room. I doubt whether any of us even breathed.

"You see, the reason for you living this particular life is to live through the grief of John's death. You were unable to get over that grief before it was suppressed by the drug and then dying, yourself. Now in this lifetime . . . once you have expressed that grief, you must let it go. That will be the final step . . . letting it go. That was the last life time in which you were together physically. Spiritually, though, you have always been together . . . and that's what really counts, isn't it?"

Pet paused again, looking at me and then at Ros and Ann, as if deciding whether she should continue. "If Lennon had lived . . . if he had not been shot, he would have begun to talk of this, somehow . . . and I get the feeling that he has confided in a friend or a member of his family, who knows why John's past had haunted him in his present."

I instantly became alert. "I do have a question. A story like this is hard to check out . . . some stuff I have. Like Katherine's birth record . . . but I'm not completely sure of John's name . . . only because I can't find a record of him in Petworth . . . I've found a record of a John Baron in Fittleworth who may be his grandfather . . . anyway, my question is . . . was his name John Baron?"

"His name was either John Baron or John Fitzherbert. Now, sometimes, I'm completely wrong with names so you'll have to look into that yourself."

'Great,' I thought, 'I'm becoming convinced of John Lennon but I'm not so sure of the name John Baron.' I mulled over the name Fitzherbert . . . I'd never heard of it, but I would add it to my list.

After thanking her and offering to pay her, she insisted, "No, I do not want money . . . your search is genuine and I am happy to have helped. When people ask me to tell them if they'll get rich or stuff like that . . . then I take their money . . ."

Pet had driven off into the night; Ros, Ann and I walked silently through the dark, winding lanes of Petworth. There was no traffic, the shops were all closed and the only sound came from the tapping of our shoes on the stone street.

Finally, Ros broke the silence asking if I was O.K. I said I was overwhelmed. Only a short time before, I was dubious about John

Baron being the same soul as John Lennon. Now, I was becoming sure. All I had to figure out now was if he was a Baron or a Fitzherbert!

Ann cut in, "Jewelle, I wanted to tell you this earlier but I could not, because Pet was there and I thought it might interfere with her reading. This afternoon, after I left you and Ros at Peter Jerrome's, I went home and something quite strange happened. My daughter, Becky, came to me in the garden ... you know, the daughter with the "gift" that I told you about this afternoon. I told her that a woman had come from Canada and was looking for information on a past life. I just said, "There's a woman here from Canada, who thinks she lived another life ... here in Petworth. A few years ago, a man was killed ... then Becky interrupted me, saying 'shot' and 'John Lennon'."

I was stunned. "Becky had seen John Lennon that quickly? You hadn't discussed it with her at all?"

Yes, she assured me, Becky had seen it all that quickly and she would have had no way of knowing anything about me and my reasons for being in Petworth. Ann repeated her reluctance about saying anything in front of Pet, but when Pet had "seen" John Lennon connected to me, as well as Becky; Ann was finding it all incredible. On my request to meet with Becky, Ann said she didn't know if Becky would. She explained, "She's very shy about her "gift" but I'll ask."

Reaching my lodging, I had the same sense of foreboding as before and was tempted to run after Ros and Ann. I made my way to my gloomy little room and collapsed on my bed.

A piercing scream awoke me. But as I sat up, the only sound in my room was the pounding of my heart. In the moon light, I saw myself reflected in the mirror. Pale skin, dark eyes and, for a moment, long dark hair. I put my hand to my head, fingering the short locks; felt a shiver run the length of my spine. Of course, my hair wasn't long. I must have seen a shadow.

105

# Eighteen

Although the arrival of morning brought me some relief, a cold chill continued to pervade me as I sat alone over early breakfast in the warm, sun-filled dining room. Barely noticing the delicious home-made marmalade and whole wheat croissants, I was deep in thought when my hostess startled me by handing me a note.

Ros, on her way to work, had left a message saying that Ann's daughter, Becky, had agreed to meet me. I would find her on the corner of Market Square at ten o'clock; I was to look for a younger version of her mother. Ros' note also told me she had arranged a meeting with Jumbo Taylor, a man very knowledgeable in Petworth's history. I was to meet him that evening at his residence, #5 Apple Lane.

The beautiful young woman awaiting me in Market Square looked like she belonged in 'Vogue Magazine', not in a small English village. Her blonde hair glowed like a halo in the bright sunshine. Somewhat reticently, she greeted me, stating that she hoped that she could be of some help; her mother had just given her scant details... a past life in Petworth and my connection with John Lennon which she had already seen.

Suggesting that we begin by walking, she led the way through the busy lanes; the brilliant sunshine warmed us as we progressed, without talking, to the opposite side of the village. Becky slowed her pace, and stated that she had a feeling we should go in the direction which she pointed out. I recognized the same alley I had walked with Ann and Ros; the one leading to the Shimmings Valley.

After a few minutes of walking along the path, over- looking the soft green valley, we approached a bench. Becky said, "My knees seem weak . . . I am getting something . . . let's sit here for awhile . . . I see a young girl with long, dark hair . . ."

Looking straight ahead but not seeing the lovely valley before us, Becky started speaking in a voice, no louder than a whisper, "I feel excitement . . . you are waiting for someone to arrive from down there."

She pointed to the traces of the old road to Fittleworth. "You are waiting for a man who comes to Petworth along this road . . . I see you waving . . . he sees you and waves back . . . there is a bond, a united love between you."

Becky stood up quickly and suggested we keep walking. I didn't say a word, afraid to break her concentration. As we walked further along the path, I noticed a sad expression and tears welling up in her eyes. "I can feel your loneliness . . . you are walking by yourself . . . he has given you bad news . . . he has to go away. You probably won't see him again . . . you are in deep despair . . . you keep looking back toward the valley, hoping to see him once more, but he has already gone."

The path suddenly turned back onto a lane but instead of taking the route back to the village center, Becky felt we should follow a road away from town. Once again we walked parallel to the beautiful valley. We came across a plain house that caught our attention.

The grey house sat at the edge of a field over-looking the valley beyond. We couldn't see the end of the house but I instantly knew it had a window at its furthest end. Becky was frightened. She didn't want to continue but I had to see the window. Becky reluctantly agreed, saying that psychically she, too, could see a window. She said that had been my room and I had spent hours just looking across the valley. Suddenly, time seemed to stop, our movements were like a dream, everything was in slow motion.

Finally, we reached the front of the ordinary house. The

107

window was gone! It had been plastered over but it's outline was still very visible. I told Becky we had to find out about the house.

An elderly woman wearing Wellingtons and an old house dress approached us from out of nowhere.

"Excuse me," I asked, trying to use my most polite tone, "could you tell us about that grey house? I noticed that the front window has been removed and plastered. I wonder why anybody would cover such a beautiful view? And could you tell us what year this house was built?"

"You young ladies needn't be poking around here asking questions. That house is from the 1800's and that's all I'm about to tell you." She put her hands on her hips, ending our conversation.

Becky and I hurried back to the road and began our journey back to the town center. Only when we were out of the woman's earshot did we burst out into nervous laughter.

I wondered what that was all about, the whole scene had seemed like a bad dream.

I knew that house definitely was connected to me, but the 1800s? I was beginning to see that Petworth possibly has many hidden secrets for me; some that may take a lifetime to uncover. This house was one of them.

We both started feeling more relaxed, as we circled back toward the village, leaving the soft green valley and the mysterious grey house behind.

We were heading in the direction of St. Mary's Church and as we walked my mind kept coming back to my suspicions about possibly having lived more than one life in southern England. I didn't question Becky about this but I kept wondering... how many lives have I lived, not only in southern England, but in Petworth?

As we approached St. Mary's Church, Becky motioned for me to follow her through the churchyard. We sat in the shade of a giant oak tree. Becky spoke again saying that many conversations between the young man and me took place here. He had many ideas to share, ideas which many other people of the day thought were mad; but I listened to him and took him seriously.

Becky's words began to be a blur. It seemed that everyone who was psychically involved with seeing my past life all had basically the same story. Sure, there was a few different aspects but the basic story was same, whether it was seen by Becky or Pet, Konni or Mom...A young couple, madly in love, small village in England, hundreds of years ago, parted tragically through the young man's death. The pain of parting so great that their love was unable to die.

Leaving the churchyard, we walked along Petworth's most ancient and only cobblestoned lane, Lombard Street, toward Market Square. I took the opportunity to ask Becky whether she was familiar with the song, 'Jealous Guy.' She was not, and I explained that when I first heard it, I had a vivid mental picture of lush green grass surrounding a milestone. In response, she told me that Petworth had had a milestone but that it had been hit by a lorry some years ago. Now a plaque had been erected in it's place. She offered to show me. This was unexpected! I hadn't thought of checking out the milestone.

What else had I forgotten? The chimes! But Becky knew nothing about chimes. I snapped a photo of the plaque which bore the simple phrase '49 miles to London.'

Becky and I walked through Market Square and stopped in Golden Square. With a puzzled look on her face, she sniffed the air. "I can smell fresh bread...but there is no smell in the air... is there?"

No, there wasn't, but I recalled that, when I was regressed by Laara, the first scene was of me, standing in that very square, carrying a basket of bread!

Becky's response to this information was a fleeting smile.

Golden Square has a book store, and I smiled when I noticed their address: "The Old Bakery!"

It occurred to me to ask Becky about one more location and we were once again on the move. We stopped across the lane from my bed and breakfast and I explained that since I had arrived, the place had given me the creeps!

Suggesting we walk around the exterior of the building, she declined my invitation to go inside, stating that something very bad had happened there. I tried to joke about the fact that I had a few more nights to spend there, but there was no smile as Becky insisted that she did not feel good about the place.

Approaching the back of the house, she pointed up to a small gabled window and said, "Right there! Something is wrong."

Unable to suppress my surprise, I told her the gabled window was where the staircase turned and led to my room and how whenever I went up those stairs, I dreaded it . . . and every day the feeling was getting stronger.

"Is that your room at the top? . . . It was *then*, too . . . you were a prisoner in that room, kept there against your will. I see an elderly woman . . . an aunt . . . My God!" Becky paused and I saw her shudder. "You died in that room!"

I was not surprised. I stared up at the building and thought that fate had brought me back to where it all had ended for Katherine James . . . her love . . . her dreams . . . her life.

After Becky departed, I wandered slowly back to Golden Square. I found a little delicatessen and purchased ginger beer and meat pies. I returned to the bench where Becky and I had sat, overlooking the Shimmings Valley. I ate lunch, indulging in fantasy. I sat alone where Katherine had sat, waiting for her love. The valley glimmered in the afternoon sun as I gazed at the ancient road to Fittleworth. My eyes swelled in tears, knowing that today no one would be travelling down the road towards me.

Wearily I left the beautiful valley, walking the long route back through the village.

I had been avoiding North Street, a winding street with ancient buildings on one side which hid the view of the sloping Shimmings Valley and faced on to the dark stone wall of the Petworth House grounds on the other. It was time I took a walk around the area. As I walked beside the renovated Thompson's Hospital I had no feelings at all. However, on the same street, a tall and narrow red brick building caught my attention. A sign said "Sommerset Hospital."

The traffic was annoying, and I felt suffocated, as I was

compelled to walk several times back and forth in front of the brick building. To me, it felt ghoulish and evil. A small porch enclosed two wooden benches and beyond, a dark heavy oak door. I recognized the door. I knocked but there was no answer. I was angry, angrier than I'd ever felt. I wanted to scream, "Open the door . . . I know you're in there." Was I angry at past ghosts or angry at my past memories that seemed to be refusing to come out?

(I have yet to solve the mystery of the hospitals. Just before leaving Petworth, I went to the library and read in an article titled "Some Buildings of Petworth" . . ." Sommerset Hospital, dating from the 16th century, has it's 'Original Door' from 1654." I knew it! Part of me wished that Becky and I had gone together to the street with the hospitals, but part of me wanted to leave well enough alone. I had been correct about the door, a door that Katherine would have seen, and again I knew there were parts of Petworth unexplainable to me, and the rattling of too many ghosts may have proved detrimental to my mental health!)

A mauve and purple dusk fell on Petworth as I knocked on the door of #5 Apple Lane, remembering Ros' words, "Jumbo Taylor is an ever so nice chap who probably knows more of Petworth's history than anyone . . ."

I introduced myself to the blue eyed, husky man. He invited me in to the warm, inviting kitchen and bade me to sit at a small oval table near the crackling stove. I explained my interest in Petworth history was confined to the period of the late 1600s. Mr. Taylor's warm and encouraging manner made me go to the heart of the matter and tell him of my certainty of having lived a past life in Petworth and of my need to check out the history of the village as a means of confirming it. I asked him if this quest of mine surprised him.

"No, I'm sure we all have many lifetimes . . . your story is no surprise at all."

Greatly relieved, I asked him if I could start asking him questions. "Did he know of the James family during the 1600s?"

He confirmed that James were a well established family in Petworth during that period.

"Did he know anything of the early history of my bed and breakfast, the Grange House?"

Part of the house had been added in the later 1700s but the original part pre-dated 1600. At one time it may have been servant's quarters for domestic help, working at Petworth House.

I told him of my confusion with Petworth House. Although I had no familiar feelings towards the massive stone house itself, I did feel connected to the many black wrought- iron plaques that lined the low corridor walls within the House.

Mr. Taylor patiently explained that the plaques were a collection of inserts from fireplaces used in the 17th Century, Katherine's time.

I was puzzled. "Why wouldn't the House be a memory; it's so gigantic, so imposing."

"When did Katherine James die?"

"1682 or 1683."

He smiled, "Petworth House was re-built in 1688; so if you are Katherine James, you wouldn't have memories of the present house. It was re-built after you had died!"

I felt in a mild state of shock as I continued to ask questions. I asked Jumbo if he might be able to identify a route or roadway if I read a description from "Katherine's Story." "They started on the road to Chichester . . . John turned the buggy into a narrow path that wandered through a lightly wooded area . . . they walked among the thin trees and what looked like a farmer's field, when all at once the earth came to an end . . . they were standing on the top of cliffs . . ."

When I asked Mr. Taylor if this made any geographical sense, he indicated that it was possible and went to fetch a map. Spreading out a large scale map of Petworth and surrounding area, he showed me the Road to Chichester. At my question, he said that was how the road was known. He showed me how one would follow that road and then turn off at a field, and that the cliffs I mentioned were probably the abandoned quarry, now grown over.

All that I had written was quite possible!

I read another part . . ." They drove this way and that, past the

112

hospital, over the little stone bridge into the country . . . wild flowers were everywhere."

Mr. Taylor looked in a drawer and emerged with another map; one of Petworth in the 1600s. He pointed out the hospital. Then he carried on to show where the ancient stone bridge had been; it had been re-built but it's original foundations were still there. The wild flowers, he stated, were probably just the foxgloves, an old variety, native to the area, which grow all over in the summer.

My head was spinning! Patrick White! Was he part of this? My dream of Patrick flashed before me . . . he had said, "Jewelle, put foxglove on my grave" . . . and of my reading with Madeline, so many years ago, Patrick had said that in time I would understand . . .

I would have to digest this all later; there was still more to hear from Mr. Taylor. I asked him about chimes. "Were there any in Petworth in the 1600s?"

Market Square had had a water clock; time was marked in intervals by the ringing of chimes. These chimes could be heard all over the village! My mother's words of five years ago were etched in my mind, "He seems to be talking about his death. Oh, and I could hear chimes; not in the song but I could hear them in my mind . . . there were chimes where you lived."

Her words faded as my sister's voice came to mind; her voice on the tape; the tape that arrived as I returned from Mere. "When you played the song 'Jealous Guy' I was aware of chimes; there were chimes in the background of where you had lived."

I was doing my best to keep my emotions in check as question after question was being answered. "Were they any asylums in the Petworth area at the time?" Mr. Taylor's response to this one was a single word answer, "Plenty."

He elaborated that, in those days, an asylum was simply a place to remove a person from society, for mental or physical reasons. Asylums did not necessarily mean a mental institution but merely a place of confinement.

(I later learned there were actual "asylum carts" that transported patients to these institutions. I remembered that my mother had mentioned John being taken away in a cart and Pet

113

had said he was taken to an asylum. I could only imagine where John may have died and I felt, hundreds of years later, sick at the thought of his pain.)

When I took my leave of the soft-spoken Englishman, I thanked him effusively for his time and his information; he verified so much more that I had ever hoped for. He assured me that the pleasure was his because he enjoyed every opportunity to talk about the history of his town, Petworth.

All was quiet at Grange House when I let myself in and crept up the stairs. The cold chill grew stronger with each step. I could feel the old woman's presence. I sat down on the top step and decided to deal with Aunt Agatha.

I hissed into the night, "Go away, Auntie! Did you think you and Rachel could hide this forever? I'm in control now. You can go to Hell!" The cold chill which had hovered above me since my arrival seemed to disappear. Whether it was a case of mind over matter or not, I was able to go to bed in relative peace.

The moon shone through the narrow window, embracing my attic room in a soft golden glow. So very long ago, had Katherine lain in this very room, as John Baron had watched over her, waiting for her to die? Tonight was he also watching and waiting; this time not for Katherine's death but for her to begin to live?

I awoke to my last day in Petworth and watched the first traces of the morning light blanketing the little town. Triumphantly, I looked around the room . . . just a room; no longer a sinister prison, guarded by a strong-willed aunt.

Another note from Ros invited me over for Sunday lunch at one o'clock. I was happy to spend my last day in Petworth with this special woman.

She wanted to know how things had gone with Becky. I was still in awe of how my day had gone with both Becky and Mr. Taylor as I shared with Ros my findings, detail by detail. Having talked to Jumbo, she already knew of the road to Chichester and the cliffs. She offered to show them to me after lunch.

"Lunch" was roast beef and Yorkshire pudding followed by a trifle for dessert. "Ros, that was the best lunch I've ever had. At

home, lunch is a sandwich and . . . oh, I'm going to miss you . . ."
I began to cry.

"Now, now, enough of that," she fussed, handing me a tissue.
"Let's go on that walk."

For the first time since my arrival, the sunshine had given way
to a light rain. As Ros and I walked through a field leading to a
trail, she pointed to where the foxglove grew each summer. All
I could do was visualize the fields a riot of color. Then I sensed
something familiar and slowed. Here were the trees along the
river and as we rounded the curve in the path, the bridge.
Shrieking, I ran to the middle of the bridge, looking back towards
Ros who was pointing out the ancient stone foundations, the only
remaining part of the original small bridge. Enormous oaks gave
way to a thin pine forest where Ros commented, "In the spring
this is known as the Bluebell Wood."

Bluebells! I'd forgotten Konni's last words as I had left for
England. "You loved bluebells." As with the foxgloves, I had
missed the season but again I had found a piece of Katherine's
past. The land suddenly seemed to have become a giant bowl. We
were standing in the middle of the ancient quarry, now grown
over in soft green. We began to climb up the steep ground;
laughing as we slipped and climbed over dead trees, finally
reaching the high ground. I turned around and gasped. The earth
looked as if it had just fallen away before us. It was all so familiar.
I could see the whole countryside, another small village in the
distance, the Bluebell Wood and the expanse of soft, rolling hills
in the distance. I saw beside us a farmer's field with the road to
Chichester in the distance. I was in Ros' arms, sobbing uncontrol-
lably with a painful kind of joy.

"I am home, Ros, I am home . . . and if I never see this beautiful
place again, I will always know where home is."

" . . . there, there, Katherine . . . Jewelle, remember that home is
where the heart is."

A veil seemed to lift, as fog would dissipate on a sunny day. I
could see Ros clearly. As clearly as I had seen Robert Philp; the
same soul as Peter Jerrome.

I thought of Ros' concern, her loving kindness as she arranged all the people who could help me rediscover my past. This person had also cared for me once long, long ago. I could only smile with delight as my eyes rested on the loving face of my dear Polly, Katherine's nanny.

Somehow, I said my farewells to Ros and to Petworth. My search was over.

I boarded the silver jet and waited to begin my journey back to my Canadian home. My eyes felt heavy as my mind sped fast motion through the events of the past week.

A passenger, directly in front of me, annoyingly rumpled his newspaper. I glanced; then I sat up taking notice of the headline — "Patrick White Dies." I stared closer. An Australian novelist. What did I expect? My Patrick White? The incident, however, has never ceased my questioning it's meaning.

Again, I replayed my week in Petworth. "Damn," I muttered as I remembered Pet's words " . . . his name could be Baron or Fitzherbert, I'm not very good with names." Groaning inwardly, I did not relish time and energy investigating Fitzherbert.

Arriving in Vancouver, I spent the night at my mother's. Retrieving a souvenir for her from my bag; she also had something for me. She had shrunk a sweatshirt; did I want it for Kristy? "Sure," I said, as I politely examined the white shirt covered with painted bunnies. Something caught my eye. I stared incredulously. A copyright symbol and written beside it, "John Baron!" My Baron or Fitzherbert question was answered!

Despite raw emotions and jet-lag, I reached for pen and paper. As a single tear slid down my cheek, I began to write, "So you think you've lived a past life with John Lennon? . . ."

# Nineteen

Months passed. I began an incredible drive to record my experiences of the past ten years. Time became a blur of words on paper. I wondered what drove me on. This still eludes me. Finally the day arrived when all had been written and recorded and I wept as if I had lost a dear friend.

The year following my trip to Petworth, I became friends with both Sara and Dihane. Sara owned the local bookstore, Dihane was my next door neighbour. Slowly I began to confide my story to both women. My memories of ridicule from Debbie soon dissipated as both women accepted the possibilities of my past life.

One afternoon Sara phoned. There was a visiting psychic in town and would I like to meet her? We could meet that night in her store.

As I entered the tiny shop, the only light came from a snow covered street lamp, casting a blue hue on the shelves of books. The night already seemed magical.

Sara and Judy waited in a small office at the rear of the store. Judy, a young woman with soft, dark eyes had a manner which immediately put me at ease.

Judy's gift is the ability to receive messages from her guides and spirits through automatic writing. Although I had read of this, I had never witnessed it and was excited and intrigued with the process.

As we got settled, Judy's observation was that I was writing a book. To my amusement, she went on to say there would be more books coming. I thought if I survived the completion of one book, I would be lucky.

After a few preliminaries, she asked me if I had any immediate concerns. I asked her to tell me about John Baron, a man I had been in love with in another life. I mentioned how an English psychic had told me, in his last lifetime he had confided in someone close to him, his recollections of a past life.

Judy responded, saying that John Baron was no longer in this world, he had passed on to the spirit world and was in a good place. He was all right. But whom did he tell about his recollections of a past life? Who knew?

Wondering what to expect, I watched Judy write in huge flowing letters, "Mother knows."

Yes, my mother knows my story, but she didn't know the person who had been John Baron. Then it hit me what "Mother knows" might mean.

John Lennon's name for Yoko was Mother! So, could "Mother knows" mean that Yoko knows?

Sensing my apprehension, but not knowing why, Judy took some time telling me not to worry. She said my story has a happy ending, in fact it was a never ending story.

Then I blurted, "Tell me about John Lennon."

Judy only looked mildly surprised as her pen began to again spell out in flowing letters, "I talk to Julian."

I swallowed hard with the realization that maybe John or some spirit was in the room. The writing resumed. "Julian talks to me. He will laugh at you (Jewelle), but tell him to check with Lucy. Yoko has seen me ... she has seen my spirit and will know this is a true message. Yoko will wonder what you want from her."

"Well," I laughed, "she probably thinks that about lots of people but it's not like I'll be discussing this with her or anything . . ."

"Yes, you will," Judy said, "you will be meeting Yoko ... I can see it in your aura."

She continued, "John says he talks to you, Jewelle...is that true?"

My head felt light as I attempted to grasp what was happening, "Yes, indirectly through my sister...and sometimes I talk to him myself...but I'm never sure if I'm getting through."

I felt as if I was entering another dimension. The little room seemed to fill with light and an enveloping love. For the first time since the streets of Petworth, I felt I was in the presence of my long lost John Baron.

Judy leaned towards me speaking slowly, "I can see John beside you...his arm is around your shoulder...remember... your story is never-ending...everything will be all right."

Days later, the short intense experience was still on my mind. I wrote a note to Judy thanking her for her reading.

Not only did I receive a reply from Judy, but messages from John.

I had told Judy nothing about my unfolding story; only that I'd had a past life with John. Again, the common thread of knowledge of Katherine and John's past shared by Pet and Becky, Mom and Konni; unfolded through Judy's letters.

Dear Jewelle,

"Hi! Thanks for your most welcome letter. I have to say I am really impressed with your project and I do see the stress it has caused and will cause, also I see you gaining strength from your work.

"I have messages for you from your soul mate. I feel like a bit of an intruder here but I will quote word for word..."

"John here, for my beloved Jewelle, arms open for you to receive. Long ago our souls were eternally connected for the development of our futures. Do not feel it necessary to see me as I was, nor should you always compare our lives to establish parallels. This seems to be a futile exercise. I ask that you listen for the present time and for the future of your existence on this earth plane, for now. Yes, I feel your frustration of the task you have chosen to get through to the people. Remember, I, too, tried in my own way to get the messages out that I received and used as songs.

For this message I will be happy to let you know that I will help you access your light within, for it is only with the faith of that which is unseen that you reach out to the faith of others. The energy must be compatible to create. Your nature is to love and to trust, but more than once I have felt your tears of frustration with the world."

"Jewelle (this is Judy) he says one more thing at the end ... 'Dance with me my beloved; John.' "

"I hope this message gives you the peace and joy as it is intended."

Your friend,
Judy


"Dance" — dance? My memories of Katherine dancing with John Baron felt again so close, so personal.

Not only did Judy have no idea that "dance" was our special connection; she had no idea of the "coincidences" that I had noticed between John and me. These similarities held a fascination for me. Now it was a relief to hear John say, " ... nor should you always compare our lives to establish parallels. This seems to be a futile exercise." It was also a verification for me that Judy was in fact speaking to him. Her familiarity with me and my story, despite not knowing me personally, was the proof I needed.

I was now having marriage problems. Bob and I, though living under the same roof, now lived separate lives. I was obsessed with writing, he was obsessed with his railway union position. I communicated with channelers, psychics and publishers; he communicated with C.P. Rail officials, Union Heads and fellow workers. However, we did not communicate with each other.

During this time, I wrote to Judy asking her to consult John for advice how to straighten out my life and feelings.

She wrote back saying, "John is your guide and soul mate, therefore cannot be impartial. However, I have sent a reading, done for you by one of my guides. I hope it will help you understand the present situation, which has it's roots in the past.

"Jewelle and Bob have chosen to do some life's work together. We see that you have lived past lives together and therefore always feel a comfort of knowing each other from the beginning (of meeting).

"Look back and within the reflection you will see that many lessons have come from both of you, not the least of which is the obvious one of proving your love for each other.

"The picture is one of you as a woman who is preparing tea for guests in a small but nicely furnished room. There is a fire in the corner of the room and a candle chandelier of sorts. The floor has a woven rug with dark red colors. The settee or place of sitting is dark. There is a bit of a commotion as guests are arriving; perhaps this is a birthday party celebration, one you have been anticipating for quite some time. We see you are surrounded by a group of peers who are whispering to you of a flirtation you are experiencing. You are flattered. However, your parents are strict and forbid any activity; you are promised in marriage to someone entirely different.

"The two men in question are indeed soul mates and indeed to this time you have not chosen between them, as they both love you and choose to be near you to learn from you and teach you. You can now tell yourself who these soul mates are; whom you love for almost opposite reasons."

Our marriage took another three years to officially die. Part of me will always love Bob and now, ironically, we, too, share a past life. A past life within this present life.

Weeks later, I officially asked Judy to do channelling from John to record, to possibly publish . . .

*March 16, 1992*

Speaking to Judy – John's answer to Judy's request to channel his messages.

"John here. Yes, as you requested, you may be a messenger for me to one who has been told of previous existences through mostly a dream state. Unlike some, who experience and truly feel through this state of being, Jewelle has chosen to pay attention to her messengers as a confirmation to herself that something better and more fulfilling awaits in the hereafter.

"Life after life after life we carry out our eternal goal of evolution, just as you are able to witness the evolution of sub species, so we are able to bear witness to our own. Jewelle and I are mates in spirit as well as in the physical and in doing so we shall help each other to experience to the fullest. Ours is a long and beneficial relationship. My wish personally is not be thought of exclusively as John Lennon, as this is a mere shell. What lies within is the essence of who I am. I fancy myself as a guide at this time as a need to sharing reincarnation recollection, vital to mankind as a whole now and in the important years to come. Good then, let's carry on with Jewelle's reading. She knows we were in touch during several lifetimes of British ancestry and her choice this time to be born in relative lacking was hasty to say the least. Not my choosing, but it is not my choice to make. She separated from me at great sacrifice to herself, in the intent of learning and not being so comfortable. The idea was perhaps that her previous lives were not teaching as they might and evolution insisted on levels of growth that drew us apart for more than one ribbon of existence. I have, of course, access to our friendship in an esoteric way and more often she was unable to remember this for her own protection."

*March 30, 1992*

"John here. Let me show you Jewelle's past lives with me. White cliffs and a hopeless romance. The days are grey and long without each other. (He says) keep my cross close to your heart so we are forever connected. Our deepest feelings are still felt this three hundred years because the soul is able to see all that has happened at once; now and in the future as well.

(Speaking to Jewelle) "Yes, I too shared the feelings remembered with those who would listen and could slow down long enough for the realizing of past lives. Cherish this as I do, we have the connection to carry on with our most gracious host and messenger. Only now will I ask you to rest as fact finder.

"You will feel my presence as long as it is acceptable for you. Your mixture of emotions shows for me as different colors surrounding you, as your thoughts form.

*April 8, 1992*

"Our Petworth. I am very happy you have made this journey. You can now see and remember the feelings there too. I felt the need to be with you, for it was us, wasn't it? Petworth is a changing and new place but it will always have the history it is rich with."

In the previous eighteen months from the time I left Petworth, I had stayed in contact with Ros and Ann. This contact was equal to that of friends everywhere, just keeping up with the latest news. On April 21, 1992, I was pleased to receive a letter from Ann. Opening it, I had no idea the letter included a communication from John.

Dear Jewelle,

"It was good to hear from you. Ros and I are writing this letter together.

"After your last letter arrived, Ros and I strongly felt we must try and get things moving again from the Petworth end. We decided to get Becky and Pet together. Pet couldn't come so Becky's friend, Sophie, came instead. She and Becky work well together in their psychic circle.

"This is what happened when we met:

"Becky and Sophie started to get to work; they went into a meditation, asking us to do the same and they said to think of you. Sophie wrote down what came out of Becky's mouth. It was really amazing! I am enclosing the piece of note paper that has all the details of what John said through Becky.

"I hope our efforts may have helped. We only wish you

could have been here that evening. It was very personal, we felt like eavesdroppers! We will have another session soon."

Fondest love,
Ann and Ros

*Channelled reading through Becky...*

First, Becky said, "I can see a shop with a Hovis sign outside it ...I can smell the bread again."

From John... "It's me again, just a different channel. The dancing hasn't stopped. Still dancing with you, just a different place. Arms around your waist with your hair smelling sweetly. Do you remember violet flowers? ... smell of hair? ... curls in hair ...ringlets and blue ribbon and blue dress. Choker round neck ...cameo. Waltz type music (Quick beat)...Dark eyes."

He came in then and said, "Hello" and "John."

Then... "This is for you, Katherine..."

"Through flowers and songs
I give her my heart
Katherine my dear
So sweet and so mild
Oh so tender my love
You are just a child."

He then says,

"Katherine, come back to Petworth, your roots are there ... we'll walk together along the road where we weren't allowed to walk, hand in hand."

Then John said, "Becky, you are so very clever; you found out about the bread."

My hands were shaking as I read and re-read the letter. I could vividly visualize these English ladies sitting one evening in a warm sitting room while a light rain fell on the surrounding green countryside. My dear, dear friends, I thought, my heart swelling with love and gratitude.

Through tears I looked out my own window and spotted my

neighbor friend, Dihane, strolling down the street. I went outside and said in what I hoped was a calm voice, "Dihane, I need to see you." However, I began to sob as I showed my neighbor the notes from Petworth. I gulped, "It's the mention of dancing... it's our own private pass word. And when he said, "Katherine, come back to Petworth"... this has always been my dream... I know it's not even possible... no one has even understood my need to do that... and when I read John's words... well, it was like I was home..."

I laughed self-consciously, "This has really shaken me up. You'd think after all that's happened the last few years I wouldn't be such a baby about all this... maybe because this came in the mail unexpectedly; I don't know. I do know that the words in this reading are all so familiar... so close... so real!"

Dihane, who had been silent, burst out with, "God damn, you don't even look like yourself... I can really see this other person in you... it's Katherine!"

A short time later another channelled reading came from Becky in the form of two poems. One poem from John and one poem from Katherine's mother. Katherine's mother? This was unexpected and I wondered how many spirits from Petworth were still around.

John says, "From lady's love who is singing...
Tree with no leaves
Where are you now?
Cut down and gone
Like the sound of our song
Long grasses in time
Sway with the breeze, follow me
Cry the tears of joy, tears of laughter
Bring me close to you from now and forever after...
Celebrate our love, 'twas true emotional love."

The spirit of Katherine's mother said, "This is how Katherine would speak to her maid..."

"Collect the horse
Take me to town
Buy me the finest silk
Make me a gown
Taffeta lace and all the trimmings
I'll be the rose of the Valley of Shimmings
Fetch my bonnet
Fasten the ribbon
Are my plaits even?"

Then, like a splash of cold water this message arrived from John, through Judy ...

"John here. My beloved Jewelle, you are so concerned about the opinions of others, often I am unable to be with you. Do you feel the need of separating us so? Please consider for a moment that I, too, have feelings and if I am unable to reach out to you, my suffering is equally great. Our love is that real, yes. It is not just a story. Our love is alive and not a fairy tale nor is it a coffee time topic. Yes, I wish the same consideration of other beings. You may be open with me if you feel I have abused our friendship, please."

I was stunned! This was not an expected message. As the first shock began to wear off, I began to sob. What was he talking about? Did I casually talk about our "story" and not take it seriously? Maybe I did. It was a way of not totally experiencing our love; for if I totally accepted it, I would have to also experience the pain as well.

I was hurt by his words. Then I was angry. Angry as Hell. I phoned Judy, asking her to bear with me. I told her I had a message of my own for John. She agreed to listen and relay my words. I began, "God damn you, John Baron, or whoever you are. I've spent over a decade of my life hunting down this "story" of ours. I've gone into debt, I've fought with Bob, fought with friends, struggled to maintain my sanity, but I never doubted our past. (Well, maybe I have.) It's pretty bloody easy for you to sit on your cloud and judge me down here on earth."

I was still steaming as I hung up the phone. Then the humour hit me. I was arguing with a spirit! Yet, for the first time I really knew how real we are. I felt both love and frustration with my situation . . . no different than what I'd felt with my relationship with Bob in our human day to day life. John had accomplished exactly what he had intended! He made me see how real this was. However, when things go bad I still find myself muttering, "Damn you, Baron, . . . you've got the easy part."

John's answer arrived soon after. "John here. Judy, please send to Jewelle, as always, my thanks, for my gratitude to her knows no bounds. I can see this pain of not knowing without a doubt that we exist is most difficult. Our asking to have faith in us and in things unseen, is in the very least overly much. Jewelle, do not look too far for your answers, they are within you and lying dormant for you to discover. Yes, I am part of you and always shall be, only occasionally I, too, feel the need to express the truth as I see it. I know all too well that my words of despair were difficult for you to hear. As I have done through time, I bend on one knee, take your hand in mine, look in your eyes and ask for your understanding and forgiveness.

Understood, I will not be as forceful again as the need for these words is done. Be with peace in your heart, my Jewelle, and once again I must say a special thanks for the merging of our story. A complete understanding of the thoughts of others is here too. We have our own growth, do we not? Our own fears and loves that may or may not disappoint the world as we know it."

A final message came through April 20, 1992: John's version of his life (or lives) with Katherine.

Judy asked John . . . "Tell me the story of John and Jewelle."

"Once upon a time. Just kidding. Okay, our lives mostly take place in the south of England. Southeast actually. We were young and truly wild for each other. Our marriage was one of beauty. We were very sociable people, with many to see, and functions of influence to attend.

"I was doing much work in a clerical way for the township as it was fashionable for me to do this. You see, much more so then, the son carried on with the father's traditions and all business was handed down from father to son.

127

"There too, our families were a great part of our doings. Visits and teas were an acceptable part of our lives. Years after I was gone, Katherine dreamed of our being together and with all I could gather, I would be there with her, my beloved.

"Yes, Katherine and Jewelle are the same, as I am John Baron or actually it was John the Baron of York descent.

(Can you describe Katherine and John?)

"First Katherine. Long auburn hair, she kept tied back and usually wore a hat or bonnet of sorts. She loved the color blue and she could often be seen from a distance picking handfuls of flowers to put around the kitchen. Mother thought maybe she was a little light-headed but I never told her. She was sensitive and easily hurt by the words of others. We enjoyed the fire and hot fresh breads.

"John is a man of considerable height, over six foot, I would say. I will visit them later. (Interesting, Judy commented.) For now, I will say he was of a spiritual nature. He believed in prayer and honesty and truth for all. Perhaps this was his downfall for he had a naiveness of belief in others that eventually cost him. But to describe him, he had a good lot of hair and very pronounced face with a large jaw. The colors of his working clothes were black and the overcoat cape-like. Not fancy really, but what was needed.

"The pain of parting was very great and really it wasn't time for us to part but we had to accept, despite our frustration. Believe me that jealousy had a great part of the situation as I had to leave."

Jealousy? 'Jealous Guy'? The song 'Jealous Guy', with chimes in the background and Katherine and John always parting; always separated.

On and on, – the thread of our story of our past lives always remains the same, yet I have so many unanswered questions, always hinted at.

Two years later. Life goes on.

Patrick White came to me again, in a dream. "Jewelle," he

128

whispered softly, "it's time to find our son." Nine months later I met Troy. Blue eyes like his father; questions Life like his mother.

For years, I often remembered Patrick's request, "Jewelle, put foxglove on my grave." Finally, on a hot July afternoon, 1994, I put a single stalk of pink foxglove on his final earthly place of rest.

Korinn takes a spell of talking to spirits on the Ouija board. She asks about Castlemere. The board tells her it did exist, pre-1900. Is this why I couldn't find a Castlemere on a modern map? She goes to the Vancouver Public Library where she finds a map, dated 1845, Lancashire. Castlemere is now part of Rochdale, Lancashire. A Ouija board gave her this information! Stranger things have happened!

Finally, thankfully, the memory of John Lennon no longer haunts me; I hear his music; I smile.

John Baron? Konni and I continue to communicate with him and why not? As in all friendships and all relationships; it's a never-ending story.

*April, 1994*

I return to Petworth. Will my heart still feel connected to this English town, or was that all a fleeting experience? I again land at Gatwick, and take a speeding train through green Sussex countryside. My soul sings, my heart cries in joy. I am at peace. Beautiful, beautiful Sussex. I am home.

The night of storms has passed
The sunshine bright and clear
Gives glory to the verdant waste
And warms the breezy air;

And I would leave my bed
Its cheering smile to see
To chase the visions from my head
Whose forms have troubled me.

—Emily Jane Bronte